FODOR'S

VIEWS TO DINE BY

Jerome E. Klein

FODOR'S TRAVEL PUBLICATIONS, INC.
New York & London

The United States

ALABAMA
BIRMINGHAM

Hugo's Restaurant

Hyatt Birmingham
at Civic Center
901 21st Street North
Birmingham
Alabama 35203
Telephone: 205–322–1234

All major credit cards
Dinner
Reservations recommended
Jacket optional
Liquor served
Dinner: $13.50 to $14.95
full 3 courses, without wine
Chef: H. Andrew Hamilton
Maitre d': Tommy Brown

The view to dine by from Hugo's is particularly nice after the sun has set and the lights of the city go on. But this is not to say that the daytime view isn't also impressive; it features important buildings such as the Museum of Fine Arts, the Jefferson County Courthouse, and several high-rise office buildings, including the Bell South Building.

The restaurant is one of the town's favorites, and has been since it opened in 1973. One local newspaper recently voted Hugo's "the best restaurant for a celebration." One of the more unusual and surprising events to occur here was when a guest videotaped his marriage proposal. Luckily, the lady said yes.

Among the menu's specialties are Artichoke Hearts, Pasta Primavera, Filet Mignon with Cabernet Sauce, Veal Florentine, Lemon Sole with Lychee and Citrus Sauce, Roast Prime Rib of Beef with Fresh Grated Horseradish, and Spit-Roasted Young Duck. A popular dessert is Hugo's Key Lime Pie.

POINT CLEAR

The Grand Dining Room at Marriott's Grand Hotel

Point Clear
Alabama 36564
Telephone: 205–928–9201

All major credit cards
Breakfast, lunch, and dinner
Reservations requested
Jacket and tie required after 6 P.M.
Liquor served
Dinner: $25 to $50
full 3 courses, without wine
Lunch: $7 to $12
Chef: Gerard Pinault
Maitre d': David Wilson

This resort has a 150-year tradition of serving its guests well. The Grand Dining Room offers local and Continental specialties and entertainment every night.

The view is of the expanse of Mobile Bay and its sailing boats and ships. If you eat breakfast early enough, you can see the boats departing for deep-sea fishing.

ALASKA
ANCHORAGE

Josephine's

Sheraton Anchorage Hotel
401 East Sixth Avenue
Anchorage
Alaska 99501
Telephone: 907–276–8700

All major credit cards
Dinner
Reservations advised
Jacket requested
Liquor served
Dinner: $26 to $40
 full 3 courses, without wine
Executive Chef: Anil Roy
Chef: Mark Linden
Maitre d': Mike Meek

Perhaps the best way to start exploring Anchorage is to have dinner at Josephine's. Here the view looking north is of Knik Arm, the port, Mt. McKinley, the Cook Inlet, and the Chugach Mountain Range. Toward the south you see most of the city of Anchorage. All this is viewed from the vantage point of the 15th floor of the hotel where the elegantly decorated (in shades of apricot and green) Josephine's is located. (If you want to sample the cuisine and the view at a lower price than a full dinner you can sit in Josephine's comfortable lounge, on the south wall.)

Josephine's menu is primarily Continental, but it leans toward *nouvelle cuisine* and is served with style. Each plate is prepared with concern for the arrangement and design of the food.

Named for the Empress Josephine, wife of Napoleon Bonaparte, this European-style restaurant has magnificent carpets and fabrics patterned after those in Napoleon's last palace. The recurring motif of the Trumpeter Swan—the emblem of Empress Josephine—serves as a reminder that this bird migrates across the Arctic. Six French-style chandeliers created in Spain add luster to the Continental decor.

A suggestion: one of the more delightful specialties of Josephine's is the *Lobster LaPagerie,* tender, moist lobster tail stuffed with shrimp mousse and baked in phyllo dough, served with champagne and cilantro sauce. Alaska is *the* place for lobster tail!

ARIZONA
TUCSON

Ventana

Loews Ventana Canyon Resort
7000 North Resort Drive
Tucson
Arizona 85715
Telephone: 602–299–2020

All major credit cards
Dinner
Reservations recommended
Jacket suggested
Liquor served
Dinner: $30 to $40
* full 3 courses, without wine*
Chef: Akram Azzam
Maitre d': Al Chija

The elegant Ventana dining room has two full walls of windows and a third wall of lustrous glass bricks lighted from behind. The view through the windows of this gourmet restaurant offers a full panorama of Tucson's skyline, the Canyon Waterfall, and the desert and mountains beyond.

Ventana is rich in its decor, with Woodmere, German Schottz Wiesel crystal, and plush seats. The colors are muted and the lighting soft. The tables, set with white linen, are illuminated by the flame of an oil lamp in the form of a clear glass disk. Each table has a crystal glass bud vase holding a single rose. Harp and violin music set a romantic ambience.

The cuisine is exceptional. A recent guest, just come from a visit to Vienna, said, "This restaurant poses a serious threat to the finest dining establishments in Europe." Chef Azzam, an American who began his cooking career in Belgium and has worked with Swiss and German chefs, says he thinks of cooking as an art. This is reflected in the appearance of his dishes, where vegetables, cut by Akram himself, are prepared and presented so beautifully that each plate is a picture of gastronomic perfection.

Akram uses reduction sauces, made by preparing the stock daily, then adding sherry, vermouth, white, burgundy, or sauvignon wines. Besides being more healthful for consumption than roux (flour) sauces, the flavor of reduction sauces is more appealing and the sauce is smoother.

The Southern Arizona Chefs Association awarded Akram a silver medal for the Ventana Medallions of Lamb in Whole-Grain Mustard Sauce. This and the Poached Sea Bass in Saffron are the favorite main dishes here. Other delights include the Mesquite-Broiled Salmon Steak with Grilled Red Onions and Chive Butter; Venison prepared in thin, tender Scallops, served with wild mushrooms and red wine sauce; Mesquite-Broiled Duckling; and Rack of Lamb with Jalapeño Jelly.

Among the desserts are Chocolate Velvet in Tulips (a fancy concoction of soft chocolate mousse under flaky pastry, with a pool of vanilla sauce laced with a raspberry swirl), and a Creme Brulée.

CALIFORNIA
BERKELEY

The Landing

Berkeley Marina Marriott
200 Marina Boulevard
Berkeley
California 94710
Telephone: 415–548–7920

All major credit cards
Breakfast, lunch, and dinner
Reservations required
Jacket recommended
Liquor served
Dinner: $10.50 to $25
* full 3 courses, without wine*
Lunch: $7 to $15
Chef: Gerry Glass
Maitre d': Nancy Webb

The Berkeley Marina Marriott, in which The Landing is located, sits directly on the San Francisco Bay shoreline. The hotel seems like a resort because of the marina setting and the lack of high-rise development in the immediate area. Yet it is only twenty minutes from downtown San Francisco.

The Landing features tiered seating so that every guest has a view. In the foreground is the Berkeley Marina with all its colorful sails, masts, and never-ending activity. In the distance one can see the entire San Francisco skyline and Golden Gate Bridge. Sunset from the restaurant is a grand experience as the sun sinks directly behind the bridge's silhouette.

The menu offers American Cuisine with an accent on seafood. Sunday brunch is offered from 10 A.M. until 2:30 P.M. with a gigantic and highly appetizing spread that keeps the guests coming back for more.

BIG SUR

Nepenthe

Highway 1
Big Sur
California 93920
Telephone: 408–624–1032 or 667–2345

All major credit cards
Lunch and dinner
Reservations not required
Jacket not required
Liquor served
Lunch and dinner: $5 to $16
    full 3 courses, without wine

Nepenthe is on a mountaintop overlooking the Pacific Ocean and the Santa Lucia mountains along the famed and scenic Highway Number One. It is 26 miles south of lovely Carmel, three miles south of Big Sur State Park, and about 165 miles south of San Francisco.

Nepenthe is a word derived from the Greek meaning "no sorrow." Many years ago, Nepenthe was used as the central setting for a motion picture, *The Sandpiper,* starring Elizabeth Taylor and the late Richard Burton; it was selected because its singular beauty and because its atmosphere were deemed a perfect setting for the story.

It's an attractive place to eat, and we like the desserts, especially the Chocolate Butter Creame Pie.

CARMEL

The Covey Restaurant at Quail Lodge

8205 Valley Greens Drive
Carmel
California 93923
Telephone: 408–624–1581

All major credit cards
Dinner
Reservations necessary
Jacket required
Liquor served
Dinner: $14 to $21
    full 3 courses, without wine
Chef: Bob Williamson
General Manager: Mr. Lynn Farrar

Just a short drive from the Carmel area of Monterey Peninsula is the delightful and tranquil Carmel Valley. It is an area protected by those who live there and love the lush verdant surroundings. Beautiful estates and excellent country clubs are quietly, privately supported by the affluent residents of the area.

One of these sanctum sanctorums can be enjoyed by those not among the area's residents. This is the Carmel Valley Golf and Country Club, on the premises of which is Quail Lodge. Within Quail Lodge is the Covey Restaurant, a gourmet establishment with seating at various levels affording both privacy and unobstructed views of a small man-made lake, glistening in perfect contrast to the subtle tones of brown, beige, and ebony

Covey Restaurant

within the restaurant. Swans float beneath a tiny bridge, adding to the setting of restful and luxuriant beauty.

The Covey Restaurant has won stars from restaurant critics for its fine cuisine. We enjoyed the Rack of Lamb and a generous selection of fresh California vegetables. We left the choice of wines to the wine steward, who selected from a variety of wines from the fine smaller vineyards with such limited production that only a few California restaurants serve their products.

LA JOLLA

The Marine Room

2000 Spindrift Drive
La Jolla
California 92037
Telephone: 619–459–7222

All major credit cards
Lunch and dinner
Reservations preferred
Jacket optional
Liquor served
Dinner: $13 to $22
  full 3 courses, without wine
Lunch: $5 to $10
Chef: Robert O'Kelly
Maitre d': Dennis Rush

One of the great views of the Pacific is to be had from the Marine Room, built right at the edge of the sea. Sometimes you think you are in the midst of the ocean and will be splashed by the breaking waves. And sometimes you find that the Pacific is not always so pacific. In fact, the Marine Room had to be rebuilt after it was destroyed by raging storms and sea in December 1982.

The cuisine here—featuring daily fresh sea bass, sole, halibut, salmon, Sea Scallops in Lobster Sauce, and other specials—has received the Taste of San Diego award. The meal is an elegant one. Appetizers range from Shrimp à la Scampi to Pacific Crab Cocktail Marina to Oysters Rockefeller. The dinner entrées are served with New England Seafood Chowder or Tossed Green Salad with Bay Shrimps and a Medley of Vegetables. Some of the Marine Room specialties include Steak Armagnac (New York steak with fresh crushed peppercorns, sautéed in French brandy), Deep Sea Scallops in Lobster Sauce, and "The Imperial Pair"—a petite filet mignon and choice lobster tail.

The Sky Room at La Valencia Hotel

1132 Prospect Street
La Jolla
California 92037
Telephone: 619–454–0771

All major credit cards
Lunch and breakfast
Reservations strongly recommended
Jacket required; tie optional
Liquor served
Dinner: prix fixe $25.50
Lunch: buffet $12
Chef: Christian Gaborit
Maitre d': Salvadore de la Torre

The Sky Room of La Valencia is situated on the 10th and top floor. From the windows of the restaurant it is easy to find yourself dreaming of sailing toward the sunset on the Pacific Ocean. The unobstructed vista of the California coastline and the La Jolla Cove and caves are all reminiscent of the French Riviera. These views can be seen from one of the ten tables in the Sky Room.

This view has been enjoyed by so many famous people that to try to list them would be an endless task. But Norma Shearer, Tennessee Williams, Audrey Hepburn, Jonas Salk, Gregory Peck, Aimee Semple McPherson, Ramon Navarro, Charles Laughton, Raymond Massey, Joseph Cotton, Herbert Marshall, Joan Crawford, Bob Hope, Groucho Marx, Greta Garbo, Mario Lanza, Zsa Zsa and Eva Gabor, June Lockhart, and Marie Wilson—shall we go on?—have been among La Valencia's guests. The luxurious La Valencia opened its beautiful wrought-iron doors in 1926 under the name of Los Apartamentos de Sevilla as an apartment hotel. It is so beautifully built and the grounds so beautifully planned and kept that the hotel and its setting must be considered part of the view.

This small dining room is in demand. Among the favorites you might consider are Salmon with Melon Sauce and Shrimp Salad served with Asparagus Tips and a special orange sauce.

LOS ANGELES

Angel's Flight Restaurant

Hyatt Regency Los Angeles
711 South Hope Street
at Broadway Plaza
Los Angeles
California 90017
Telephone: 213–683–1234

All major credit cards
Lunch and dinner
Reservations recommended
Jacket suggested
Liquor served
Dinner: $16 to $20
full 3 courses, without wine
Lunch: $9 to $17
Chef: Wolfgang Wildoer

Angel's Flight is the revolving restaurant on the rooftop of the Hyatt Regency in Los Angeles. It makes a full revolution once every hour and offers a 360-degree view of Los Angeles. From this height, Los Angeles seems to go on forever.

Angel's Flight

The menu is less varied than that of Pavan, the hotel's other restaurant. Here the specialties include a diversified salad menu and a fish of the day; there is also an exotic drink menu. The restaurant is open from 11 A.M. until midnight and is a favorite romantic spot as well as a popular place for cocktails at sunset.

The Dining Room and Outdoor Terrace
of the Hotel Bel-Air

701 Stone Canyon Road
Los Angeles
California 90077
Telephone: 213–472–1211

All major credit cards
Breakfast, lunch, dinner, and
* Sunday brunch*
Reservations necessary
Jacket required
Liquor served
Dinner: $25 to $35
* full 3 courses, without wine*
Lunch: $15 to $20
Chef: Joseph Venezia
Maitre d': Albert de Kerazan

The Hotel Bel-Air's restaurant, a popular setting for hotel guests and nearby residents, is at the end of one of the graceful arcades in the hotel's Mission-style main building. It was recently redecorated by designers Louis Cataffo and Betty Garber, with walls upholstered in peachy beige and enhanced with original art, carpeting in beige with moss green floral patterns, spacious booths covered with waffle-finish beige leather, and country-inspired Queen Anne armchairs.

Under the direction of Chef Venezia, the cuisine reflects the traditions of California, France, and even the Orient, and emphasizes fresh ingredients and artful preparation.

The dining room is neatly tucked into a corner of the plush grounds of the hotel and for the past forty years has been the most romantic setting for dining in Los Angeles. It is not unusual for celebrity neighbors living in Bel-Air to be seated next to a young visiting couple here to enjoy the surroundings and magnificent food.

For guests who like alfresco dining in warmer weather, tables on the bougainvillea-draped terrace next to the restaurant overlook the hotel gardens and Swan Lake, providing the best view to dine by in Los Angeles.

The cuisine features interesting combinations made with fresh local foods and pastas. For example, there is the appetizer of Sweetbreads sautéed with basil noodles, arugula, and shittake mushrooms. Among the favorite entrées are Mesquite-Grilled Spot Prawns on Tomato and Cucumber, Medallions of Veal with Onion Marmalade and Port Wine Sauce, Smoked Seafood with Rye Toast (tuna, salmon, sturgeon, sea bass, and mussels arranged with a display of capers, lemon, and a *trompe l'oeil* egg), Roast Sliced Canadian Duck, and Grilled Loin of Lamb with Poached Garlic and Spinach.

And the desserts! Have you ever heard of Poached Cheesecake (it's like a cream cheese mousse) with Raspberry Sauce? Other unique offerings are the herb-scented sorbets. But for chocolate lovers this is paradise. Our favorites are Chocolate Truffle Cake and Chocolate Mousse Cake! There is also Almond Kirsch Cake decorated with currants on the stem, blueberries, and blanched almonds. Decisions!

On Sunday, a delightful brunch is served from 11:30 A.M. until 2:30 P.M. that costs between $13 and $16.

The after-dinner stroll on some parts of the eleven-and-a-half acre enclave is a must. It is hard to believe that the hotel is so close to the bustle of Los Angeles. In the lower garden, the Mission-style bell tower overlooks a romantic lake whose swans add a touch of elegance. What is now the hotel was originally the offices in the early 1920s of Alphonzo E. Bell, the developer of the luxury residential community of Bel-Air. In the 1940s it was transformed into a luxury hotel that immediately became a favorite of the residents because of its refined tranquility. The residents have taken a proprietary interest in it ever since and nervously watched its recent renovation. Fortunately, in the hands of the Rosewood Hotels Organization, nothing was destroyed, only freshened and enhanced.

Dining Room and Outdoor Terrace, Hotel Bel-Air

Top of Five

Westin Bonaventure
404 S. Figueroa Street
Los Angeles
California 90071
Telephone: 213–624–1000

All major credit cards
Lunch and dinner
Reservations recommended
Jacket recommended
Liquor served
Dinner: $25 to $30
  full 3 courses, without wine
Lunch: $8 to $15
Chef: Werner Glur
Maitre d': Tom Berning

There are two viewing possibilities here, one from the restaurant and another from the cocktail lounge. On the 35th floor of the Westin Bonaventure is the Top of Five, a restaurant with a 360-degree view of Los Angeles and beyond. At night it is particularly beautiful because of the endless sea of glittering lights. Viewing is even more fun from the BonaVista, a revolving cocktail lounge located just one flight below the Top of Five's dining room. It is even fun getting to it, down a grand staircase from the restaurant.

The Top of Five has just been beautifully redecorated. Instead of the original beige and terra-cotta color scheme, there is an updated mauve and blush decor. The tabletops in the restaurant and the lounge are made of polished black Belgian marble. The bar top is polished black granite. The original continuous bench seating that lined the perimeter of the Top of Five has been replaced with intimate booth seating without obstructing any of the view.

Chef Werner Glur has been named Chef of the Year by the California Restaurant Writers Association. His current menu features such items as mesquite-grilled Swordfish Steak Louisiana with Jumbo Shrimp and Cajun Hot Sauce, Yellowtail with Cucumber and Ginger Shoots, and Crabmeat and Oyster Fettucine. Chef Glur has taken "the fire of Louisiana Cajun cooking and mixed in timeless Szechuan recipes, creating a new spirited cuisine with East meeting West."

Lunch is served Monday through Friday, brunch on Saturday and Sunday, and dinner and cocktails are served seven days a week. The Top of Five guarantees that your dinner there will take no more than 45 minutes from arrival until departure. If they miss, they pay the check!

MONTEREY

Conservatory Room at the Sardine Factory

701 Wave Street
Monterey
California 93940
Telephone: 408-373-3775

All major credit cards
Dinner
Reservations recommended
Jacket preferred
Liquor served
Dinner: $17 to $29.50
  full 3 courses, without wine
Chef: Doug Robertson
Manager: Jeffrey Lesker

The Sardine Factory is located on historic Cannery Row on the Monterey Peninsula and has won awards for its cuisine and decor. Started by Ted Balestreri and Bert Cutino in 1968, it has collected a long list of honors, including the *Travel/Holiday* Magazine Award since 1971, the *Restaurants and Institutions* Magazine Ivy Award, *Nation's Restaurant News* Hall of Fame Award, the *Mobil Travel Guide* Award, and others.

In addition to the original dining room, there are four other dining areas. Among them are the Victorian-styled Captain's Room, with fireplace and crystal chandeliers, the Wine Cellar, an elegant lower-level room with medieval decor featuring many collector's items as furnishings, and the Conservatory Room.

Conservatory Room

The distinctive Conservatory Room is entirely covered by a glass dome and offers a unique turn-of-the-century garden setting. The room, with its green and white decor and plants in Roman containers, is dominated by a white iron crystal chandelier from Czechoslovakia and a central fountain topped with a statue of the *Birth of Venus* adapted from the famous Botticelli painting. The view to dine by is of the enclosed garden patio.

Among the menu favorites are Abalone Cream Bisque, Monterey Bay Prawns, Abalone, and, for dessert, Pear Cardinal.

Be sure to see the Wine Cellar Room with its 25-foot long banquet table, cognac bar, and tobacco humidor built by Craig Clark, a wine captain, from a 1,000-year-old redwood tree.

Ferrante's Restaurant and Bar

Monterey Sheraton Hotel
350 Calle Principal
Monterey
California 93940
Telephone: 408–649–4234

All major credit cards
Lunch and dinner
Reservations suggested
Jacket not required
Liquor served
Dinner: $8.95 to $16.95
*   full 3 courses, without wine*
Lunch: $5.95 to $10.95
Chef: Paul Gelose
Maitre d': Doug McCall

When natural pressure forced the coastal mountain range of the Monterey Peninsula into the waters of the Pacific, it created what has been described as one of the world's most dramatic meetings of land and sea.

At Ferrante's, on the tenth and highest floor of the Monterey Sheraton, this spectacular panorama comes with the meal. From here you have 270 degrees of view, which is a great deal for the eyes to digest. In the daylight hours you may see the colorful spinnakers of sailboats in regatta, the spray of migrating gray whales, and the far-away Santa Cruz mountains, changing colors with the seasons and the setting sun.

As evening approaches, the fishing fleet comes through the dusk to anchor and a quiet

settles on the shore. Lights begin to twinkle at the Fisherman's Wharf, over the Presidio, and on the streets of Old Monterey far below. The view is all-inclusive—the Cannery Row and Tortilla Flat areas of Steinbeck fame, the mist-shrouded pines of the Peninsula hills, and the magnificent Monterey Bay.

Regular visitors to Ferrante's have stories to tell of the ever-changing views—of storms rolling in off the Pacific, or the night that meteors lit up the southern sky with a brightness almost like daylight. They also might talk of the familiar faces they saw, such as Clint Eastwood, Joan Fontaine, or John Travolta, or of the old Italian families that made Monterey the colorful fishing community immortalized by Steinbeck's writing.

The restaurant is appropriately named for Pietro Ferrante, a Monterey Bay fisherman. Even he might have difficulty in deciding what to select from the *antipasti, minestre, insalate tramezzini, frittate, pasta,* and *carnie e pesci* that Chef Paul Gelose includes on his menu.

Specialties include Seafood Fettucine with succulent scampi, scallops, and clams sautéed in a light cream sauce and served with spinach fettucine. Another favorite is Shrimp Pomodoro. This delightful restaurant specializes in Northern Italian cuisine, and so, not surprisingly, is popular with the area's Italians. Desserts feature freshly baked items and delightfully rich and creamy gelato.

MORRO BAY

The Inn at Morro Bay

Morro Bay
California 93442
Telephone: 805–722–5651

All major credit cards
Breakfast, lunch, dinner, and
Sunday brunch
Reservations necessary
Jacket not required
Liquor served
Dinner: $15 to $17
full 3 courses, without wine
Lunch: $6 to $13
Chef: James G. Magee II
Maitre d': Esteban DeLuque

Here you get some clues as to why the California coast is like it is. The volcanic rock of Morro Bay juts out into the Pacific; you can't completely walk around it, nor can you climb it. Some have tried and found themselves stranded for a while. It is an unusual formation and you find yourself studying it. Many, armed with camera or paintbrush, have tried to capture it artistically. Others run to the nearest library to consult a geology textbook.

When we first wrote about this view, it was from a small modest lodging called the Golden Tee. Now, completely new and replacing it is the Inn at Morro Bay, a delightful place to dine and stay.

You begin your viewing and dining experience with a stop in the cocktail lounge, where you have a great view of the ocean and the local fishing boats. Don't worry about losing the view once you go to the dining room—from there you can see the volcanic rock formations in the Pacific Ocean, framed beautifully by eucalyptus trees. Chef Magee offers California cuisine with French overtones. The dining is accompanied by soft classical music, in keeping with the tranquil setting of the inn. Among the favorite main dishes are *Canard Roti du Soire* (fresh Roasted Boneless Duckling served with a sauce of that evening), *Pasta El Encanto* (fresh Sautéed Shellfish on Spinach and Egg Fettucini in Lobster Bisque), and *Saumon Moutarde* (fresh Salmon poached in Cream, served in White Wine Dijon Mustard Sauce). The desserts are all tantalizing French pastries.

The dining room is open for breakfast at 7 A.M. Dinner is ready at 5 P.M. Sunday brunch is served from 10 A.M. until 2 P.M.

The view is getting even better. This year a marina at the inn will be completed, and then you will be able to see guests arrive for dinner, or a stay, by yacht. The Inn at Morro Bay is a favorite eating place for both residents and visitors, some of whom come for dinner and decide to stay a few days to enjoy the view.

PASADENA

Skylights

The Pasadena Hilton
150 South Los Robles Avenue
Pasadena
California 91101
Telephone: 818–577–1000

All major credit cards
Lunch and dinner
Reservations necessary
Jacket required
Liquor served
Dinner: $19.75 to $25
 full 3 courses, without wine
Lunch: buffet $9.75
Chef: Hermann Thoni
Maitre d': Denis Regnier

Pasadena is that famous California city known for its annual Tournament of Roses Parade and for the Rose Bowl, the football classic. It is also an important cultural city, home to the California Institute of Technology and its NASA jet propulsion laboratory, the Huntington Library and Art Gallery, four museums, and several magnificent gardens.

The restaurant atop the Pasadena Hilton, Skylights, provides a magnificent view of Pasadena. The view at night is particularly delightful as the lights seem to extend forever. On a clear night the lights of Los Angeles, only eight miles away, as well as those of Glendale, ten miles away, are visible as well.

José Lopez, director of Food and Beverages at the hotel, is proud of the French cuisine served in this lovely penthouse restaurant. He points out that the best possible ingredients are obtained for each dish; if not available locally, he stressed, they are flown in from England, France, or from anywhere else necessary to get what is required. Among the awards received by Skylights are the Epicurean, three stars from the *Mobil* guide, and two stars from the California Restaurant Association.

Favorites from the kitchen include *Tournedos Arlequin, Filet de Fletan Biarritz,* and *Escalopes de Veau a l'Estragon.* Among the desserts we recommend are Chocolate Mousse and Creme Carmel. There are excellent French pastries as well. Sunday brunch is very popular here.

SAN DIEGO

Sheppard's
in the
Sheraton Harbor Island East
1590 Harbor Island Drive
San Diego
California 92101
Telephone: 619–692–2255

All major credit cards
Dinner
Reservations required
Jacket required
Liquor served
Dinner: $25 to $40
full 3 courses, without wine
Chef: Cindy Black

Sheppard's

This exceptional restaurant was the final project in the $30 million renovation and addition to the 750-room Sheraton Harbor Island East Hotel. It was opened in September 1984, and thanks to the remarkable Chef Black, Sheppard's is considered the best restaurant in San Diego and possibly in all of California.

The complex is located on Harbor Island, in the middle of scenic San Diego Bay. The small, elegant restaurant looks out across the Harbor Island Marina, with its colorful boats. Generally, Sheppard's diners have a view through treetops of the garden. If you want to enjoy the water view, when you make your reservation ask for a window table on the right side (as you enter) of the restaurant. Some say the view of the interior of the restaurant is even more spectacular than the outdoor view. The restaurant is decorated in soft shades of coral, accented by live green plants and matching pin cushion protea flowers which grace the centers of the tables. In the Vintage Room, a private dining room without a view that is very much like a dining room in a fine home, are six fabulous oil paintings by Nancy Bowen, a local artist, depicting Monet's summer gardens in France. This room is available for parties of four to nine people.

Cindy Black, the chef, has generated a lot of excitement. She's only 28 years old, but she knows food and good cooking as well as any older master. Her father is a diplomat and was her first cooking teacher. Her formal cooking education came from Madeleine Kamman, who runs her Modern Gourmet Cooking School in Newton Centre, Massachusetts. Cindy worked as a cook in the southwest of France after finishing school. Robert Brody, executive chef at the Sheraton, met her when she worked briefly at Apley's Restaurant in Boston. When the hotel in San Diego was looking for a chef that would fit in with the French "country" theme and decor of the Sheppard's Restaurant they were about to complete, Brody recommended Black for the job. Sheppard's opened under her direction on January 28, 1983; in 1984, Cindy Black and Bob Brody were married, and everybody there celebrated "the wedding of two cuisines."

There is ample reason for joy—the cuisine is terrific. It has been awarded the 1985 *Travel/Holiday* Fine Dining Award and has garnered praise from all California critics. Among the many delights are Duck Confit Salad, Grilled Marinated Swordfish with Coriander, Loin of Lamb with Glazed Green Beans, Fresh Salmon with Lemon-Thyme Sauce, Scallops with Sage Butter and Roe, and Snapper with Chervil. The desserts are outstanding, among them Raspberry and Chocolate Marjolaine, Apricot Tart with Marinated Dried Apricots in Puff Pastry Shell with Pistachios, and our favorite, Belgian Chocolate Ice Cream.

SAN FRANCISCO

Chic's Place

202 A—Pier 39
San Francisco
California 94133
Telephone: 415-421-2442

All major credit cards
Breakfast, lunch, dinner, and
Sunday brunch
Reservations not necessary
Dress: casual
Liquor served
Dinner: $11 to $15
full 3 courses, without wine
Lunch: $7 to $9
Chef: Joel Theriault
Proprietors: Chic Watt and George Martinez

Here's a delightful restaurant on Pier 39, San Francisco's picturesque shopping and dining tourist mecca. Even though reservations are unnecessary, you might want to phone ahead for a window table if you'd like to dine with a view.

But even if you don't see the outside view, you'll still enjoy the grand interior of this place. It was designed at considerable expense to recreate the style of old San Francisco. A marble-topped bar with brass rail is backed by artist-commissioned mirrors which go all the way from the entrance area to about halfway around the dining room. The lighting is gentle and the heavy green carpeting with the white tablecloths, silk flowers, and shaded candleholders, all contribute to a turn-of-the-century decor.

The style here is Art Nouveau. One of the interior's highlights is a painting of one of Mucha's ladies set off by smoky persimmon walls; Mucha was also the inspiration for the designs on the hand-sanded mirrors and the glass partitions. Antique buffs will like the floral-design of the chandeliers and the hand-carved sideboard. Through the beveled, hand-carved windows guests may watch boats slowly crossing the bay or people meandering down Fisherman's Wharf.

The view inspires most patrons to order seafood. The Chef's Special Dinner is guaranteed to satisfy; it features Grilled Salmon, Sautéed Prawns, Fried Scallops, Petrale Sole, and Oysters Rockefeller, accompanied by Potatoes Anna and salad or soup. The Broiled Red Snapper is also great. If you're more of a landlubber, there are veal and steak entrées.

Compadres Mexican Bar and Grill

Ghirardelli Square
900 Northpoint
San Francisco
California 94109
Telephone: 415–885–2266

MasterCard, Visa
Lunch and dinner
Reservations recommended
Jacket preferred
Liquor served
Dinner: $15 to $25
  full 3 courses,
    without wine
Chef: Agustin Iniquez
Manager: Pat Dulin

Late in 1985, the third of four Compadres Mexican Bar and Grill restaurants opened in San Francisco, atop what had been an old chocolate factory building, in Ghirardelli Square.

The square is now a delightful, fun-filled shopping complex and restaurant center, but only some of the restaurants have grand views of San Francisco Bay—Compadres has one of the best because it is higher than all the others.

Compadres is an airy restaurant decorated with cushioned wicker furniture, plenty of green plants, and an outstanding array of Mexican artifacts. There is an outdoor patio with a freestanding adobe fireplace and tables set under gas lanterns. The antique wood furniture and festive umbrellas add to the setting.

Critics praise the cuisine here. Some of the more popular items feature Potato Nachos made from thick Maui potato chips and topped with cheese, salsa fresca, guacamole, sour cream, fresh bacon pieces, and chopped scallions.

Another specialty is Chili *Rellenos,* which are freshly roasted and peeled before being stuffed with Monterey Jack cheese, Mexican *chorizo* (sausage), Dungeness crab, and other delights. The Shrimp (*camarones*) *Fajitas* are especially popular, made with marinated Gulf shrimp sautéed with onions and green peppers and then wrapped by the diner into soft tortillas. Some people like the Compadres platter, a generous combination starting with a Caesar Salad tossed tableside and followed by *Flautas,* Baby Back Ribs (smoked), Chili *Rellenos, Pollo Borracho,* and *Fajitas.*

One of the most popular and creative desserts here is the Apple *Chimichanga,* which features brandied apples in a deep-fried flour tortilla topped with vanilla ice cream and/or cheese. Also on the menu is a wonderful Taco Split, a golden fried tortilla boat filled with fresh bananas, ice cream, fruit topping, macadamia nuts, and a cherry. The Caramel Flan and Kahlua Parfaits are also very popular.

The Crown Room

29th floor
Fairmont Tower
Fairmont Hotel
Atop Nob Hill
San Francisco
California 94106
Telephone: 415–772–5000

All major credit cards
Lunch, dinner, and Sunday brunch
Reservations recommended
Jacket advised
Liquor served
Dinner: $22.50 adults
   $16.50 children
Lunch: $17.50 adults
   $12.50 children
Sunday brunch: $17.50 adults
   $12.50 children
Chef: Kurt Kratschmar

The Crown Room, perched atop the Fairmont Tower on the 29th floor, has a sweeping panorama of San Francisco Bay, the Golden Gate Bridge, the Marin County headlands, Alcatraz Island and its famed prison, the Bay Bridge, the Financial District skyscrapers, and the hills of South San Francisco. The Crown can be reached by inside tower elevators for the more squeamish, or by the glass enclosed Skylift, an outdoor elevator providing a magnificent view of the city all the way up.

Inside the Crown, guests can have their views from the tables in the revolving bar carousel in the center of the room, if they wish. It makes a complete revolution every 17 minutes.

The Crown Room features a magnificent buffet, offering over forty salads, entrées, and desserts. Cold buffet items for lunch and dinner include six prepared cold salads with such items as sliced tomatoes, sliced cold cuts, artichokes, mushrooms, pasta, coleslaw, tossed greens, Bay shrimp, poached salmon, assorted pâtés, sliced duck, sliced Cornish game hen, and roast beef. Typical hot luncheon and dinner items include London Broil with Sauce Bordelaise, Sautéed Fillet of Salmon, Baked Sea Bass Portuguese, Osso Bucco, and Fillet of Sole Amandine. Cheeses, raisins, and walnuts are there, along with fresh seasonal fruits. Dessert items include Lemon Chiffon Pie, Banana Cream Pie, assorted French pastries and more. Sunday brunch adds Pancakes Oscar, Eggs Benedict, and Cheese Blintzes.

The Crown is open daily for lunch from 11:30 A.M. to 2:30 P.M.; dinners are from 6 P.M. to 10 P.M.; cocktails are from 11 A.M. to 2 A.M. Holiday and Sunday brunches are usually offered at 10 A.M., noon, and 2:30 P.M.

Kurt Kratschmar, the Fairmont executive chef and chef of the Crown, was born and raised in Vienna and has been at the Fairmont for six years; previously he worked at various Las Vegas hotels.

People from all over the world and from all walks of life come to the Crown Room, including such celebrities and dignitaries as Claudette Colbert, Phyllis Diller, Sean Connery, the late Rock Hudson, Ella Fitzgerald, King Gustav of Sweden, John D. Rockefeller, and Alexander Haig.

Dante's Sea Catch

Pier 39
Box 213
San Francisco
California 94133

All major credit cards
Lunch and dinner
Reservations not required
Jacket not required
Liquor served
Dinner: $7.95 to $23.95
full 3 courses, without wine
Lunch: $4.95 to $11.95
Chef: Daniel Comforti
Maitre d': Scott C. Bridges

The panoramic view through the wall of windows at Dante's Sea Catch encompasses both old and new, natural and manmade splendors. From the San Francisco skyline with its historical Coit Tower and the modern TransAmerica building (called by some the pyramid with ears) to the expansive bay where sailboats are forever gliding among the luxury liners, the vista is an ever-changing painting of mood and light, vibrant by day, alluring by night.

Dante's Sea Catch

In its seven-year history Dante's Sea Catch on Pier 39 has prided itself on serving the finest and freshest seafood, pastas, and other specialties that, by combining the traditional with the unique, reflect the nature of the view to dine by. Award-winning Chef Comforti won first prize for his Crab Cioppino dish during a national Crab Cooking Olympics, and his clam chowder was honored as the very best at the San Francisco Fair and Exposition.

Certainly among the menu favorites are his Crab *Nouvelle Cuisine,* the Silver Dollar Scallops, and Prawns *Fra Diablo.* The food has to be good here—the Sea Catch is one of the 23 original restaurants on Pier 39 which is still in business.

The setting at Dante's Sea Catch is casually elegant, with its long, curving Art Nouveau dining room looking out over the marina and its colorful boats. Stained glass and Victorian lamps add to the ambience. The same green and amber color scheme in the main room is found upstairs at the bar, where guests can relax with a drink and either admire the view or just stare into the flickering flames of the fireplace.

The Mandarin

Ghirardelli Square
900 North Point Street
San Francisco
California 94109
Telephone: 415-673-8812

All major credit cards
Lunch and dinner
Reservations recommended
Jacket optional
Liquor served
Dinner: $15 to $25
     full 3 courses, without wine
Lunch: $10 to $15
Chef: Teh Ko
Maitre d': Linsan Chien

Dining in this superb Chinese restaurant is a delight partly because of the delightful view of San Francisco Bay but even more so for the authentic and beautifully served Chinese cuisine.

The original Mandarin restaurant was opened in San Francisco years ago by Cecilia Chiang and achieved its renown as the first restaurant in the United States to serve the dramatic and now very popular dishes of Szechuan and Northern China. Born and bred in Peking, Ms. Chiang opened her first restaurant in Tokyo simply because she could not find the good food to which she was accustomed. Today she commutes twice weekly between Los Angeles and San Francisco to make certain that the quality of the cuisine in her restaurants meets her rigid standards.

The cuisine here has won many awards, including five stars from the *Mobil Travel Guide* and the *Travel/Holiday* Magazine Award. Among the favorites, and there are too many to list, are Minced Squab, Peking Duck, Beggar's Chicken, Smoked Tea Duck, Prawns Szechuan, and Sweet and Sour Fish. For dessert, try the bananas dipped first in molten sugar and then in ice water to form a brittle sugar crust. A scrumptious discovery!

The pleasure of dining here is enhanced both by the view of San Francisco Bay and the exquisite Chinese furnishings. The Mandarin's many rooms are divided by screens of openwork tile or intricately carved wood. The floors are laid with jade and blue tiles and covered with colorful Oriental rugs. On the walls are needleworks done in the "Forbidden Stitch" (so called because the threads are so fine that the artisans stitching these used to go blind!). One delight is an impressive lotus blossom sculpture, handcarved and assembled from seventeen pieces of a unique light-colored Oriental wood.

Neptune's Palace Seafood Restaurant

Pier 39
P.O. Box 3730
San Francisco
California 94119
Telephone: 415-434-2260

All major credit cards
Lunch, dinner, and brunch
Reservations advised
Dress: casual elegant
Liquor served
Dinner: $9.95 to $25
     full 3 courses, without wine
Lunch: $7.95 to $25
Chef: Kevin Sadlier

Neptune's

This restaurant, too, has a magnificent view of San Francisco Bay and all of its activities. General Manager Jeanne Cambra tells of a single day of viewing in October 1985:

Fleet Week began at that time in San Francisco with ten to 15 U.S. Navy ships and aircraft carriers sailing in under the Golden Gate Bridge at 10:30 A.M., with the Blue Angels performance on the water of the Bay following at 11:30. The Coast Guard was all over the Bay that day keeping sailboats out of the pathways of the Blue Angels. Later that afternoon, just 30 feet off the end of the Pier and directly in front of our windows, a sailboat capsized and sank completely within 15 minutes. Fortunately all on board were unharmed.

As you see, this is often an exciting view to dine by.

The cuisine here has won a variety of awards, among them the silver award in the Baltimore Crab Olympics and the Overall Grand Prize at the New York Landing Seafood Festival. Favorite entrées include Baked Salmon with Three Cheeses and Swordfish Kontiki, and, for dessert, Chocolate Torta with Fresh Raspberry Sauce.

Neptune's Palace's location is exciting, too. Situated near the end of the pier, it is surrounded by the bustling activity of the pier itself. Pier 39, which opened on October 4, 1978, is an exciting collection of shops, restaurants, marinas, docks, and much more—a full-fledged entertainment center for tourists and San Franciscans alike.

One-Up

Hyatt on Union Square
345 Stockton Street
San Francisco
California 94108
Telephone: 415-398-1234

All major credit cards
Lunch, dinner, and Sunday brunch
Reservations recommended
Jacket required at dinner
Liquor served
Dinner: $28
  full 3 courses, without wine
Lunch: $18
Chef: Jeff Moogk
Maitre d': Ramona Lashley

The Hyatt on Union Square has a restaurant on top of its penthouse, thus the restaurant's name: One-Up. It offers a thrilling view of the key landmarks of San Francisco, including Coit Tower, the Transamerica building, Alcatraz Island, and the Golden Gate Bridge.

One-Up was refurbished in 1983 by Denis Allemand and Associates Design, Inc., of Los Angeles. It was given an elegant decor with a pale blue and mauve interior, accents of brass, contemporary furnishings, and an Asian influence through the use of original artworks.

Under the direction of Executive Chef Moogk and One-Up Chef Ted Rowe, the One-Up menu features New American cuisine at its finest. It offers creative, light, and exquisitely prepared dishes using the freshest, most tender regional products in addition to lots of seafood from San Francisco Bay. Cooking time is short, sauces are light, and the food is artfully presented. There is a fine wine list, including the new Hyatt Cuvee Domain Chandon sparkling wine available by the glass or bottle.

An elaborate champagne brunch is served every Sunday featuring eggs, omelets, oven-warm breads, flaky pastries, breakfast meats cooked to perfection, imported pâtés and cheeses, and the freshest fruits of the season.

The One-Up Restaurant is open for lunch Monday through Friday from 11:30 A.M. until 2 P.M. Dinner is daily from 6 P.M. until 10:30 P.M. Sunday brunch is from 10:30 A.M. until 2 P.M.

Two suggested entrées are Warm Salad of Mixed Baby Lettuce with Sautéed Lobster, Sea Scallops, and Salmon with Mango-Walnut Vinaigrette and Sliced Loin of Lamb with Comfit of Eggplant, Red Pepper Relish, Sweet Garlic, and Rosemary Natural Jus.

Among the tempting desserts are Puff Pastry Filled with Fresh Berries in Caramel Sauce and Creme Brulée au Grand Marnier. Best of all are the soufflés, either raspberry or pistachio.

Top of the Mark

Mark Hopkins Intercontinental
Number One Nob Hill
San Francisco
California 94106
Telephone: 415-392-3434

All major credit cards
Sunday brunch; cocktail lounge
at other times
Reservations recommended
Jacket requested
Liquor served
Sunday brunch: adults $19.50
children under 12: $12.50
Chef: Tony Breeze
Manager: Steve Rice

Only on Sunday is this a view to dine by. On weekdays it is a view to drink by. The Top of the Mark is in this book simply because it is a great viewing spot, and because it is probably one of the best-known vantage points in San Francisco, and has been so for many years.

The Top of the Mark opened on May 11, 1939, and since then more than 25 million people from all parts of the world have come to view all of San Francisco from its lofty perch 257 feet on top of Nob Hill and 537 feet above sea level. Not only can one see the city of San Francisco, but in addition seven surrounding counties, mountains along the Pacific Coast, three giant bridges (including the Golden Gate), and the Pacific Ocean are all seemingly within your grasp. It is a 50-mile panorama that has few to equal it in all the world.

From the time it opened as a hotel in 1926 until 1936, the 19th floor (now the Top) was the private apartment of D.C. Jackling, a copper magnate. The floor was built to his specifications with unusually high ceilings to accommodate his prize collection of mammoth oil paintings. When Jackling moved to his country estate in 1936, George D. Smith, builder, owner, and general manager of the Mark Hopkins, decided to build a skyroom bar.

Timothy Pfleuger, San Francisco's leading architect of that era, created a room in which all four walls were actually huge glass panels—especially designed to withstand 120-mile gales (no winds have ever reached this velocity in San Francisco).

The Top of the Mark reopened during the year of the San Francisco World's Fair, in 1939, but it was World War II that gave the Top its worldwide reputation. Hundreds of thousands of Allied servicemen shipped through San Francisco, and the Top of the Mark became their figurative Port of Embarkation. It was the last place they remembered and the first they wanted to come back to; as servicemen met and passed each other on Pacific fronts, the watchword was "meet you at the Top of the Mark."

When the war ended, the United Nations Charter Conference came to San Francisco. The diplomats and other dignitaries were charmed by the Top of the Mark and its grand panorama. Anthony Eden used to have his morning tea there, all alone, gazing at the magnificent view, before departing for each day's work of attempting to build a charter for world peace.

The lavish buffet is different each Sunday, and features hot and cold entrées with a great selection of appetizers and desserts as well. It is a favorite spot for local residents to take their first-time San Francisco visitors to get a bird's eye view.

Vannelli's Seafood Restaurant

Pier 39
Box 210
San Francisco
California 94133
Telephone: 415–421–7261

All major credit cards
Lunch and dinner
Reservations not necessary
Jacket not required
Liquor served
Dinner: $8.75 to $22.50
*   full 3 courses, without wine*
Lunch: $4.50 to $12.50
Chef: Claus B. Iversen
Maitre d': Tucker Short

Located at the end of Pier 39, overlooking the Golden Gate Bridge, the Bay Bridge, and all three of the Bay islands—Angel, Yerba Buena (Treasure Island), and Alcatraz— the V-shaped Vannelli's has a spectacular 180-degree panoramic view. The yacht marina just below the restaurant is always busy and interesting to watch, as are the incoming and outgoing cruise ships.

The cuisine here includes a vast selection of fresh and specially prepared seafood, meat, and poultry dishes. Among the popular entrées are Shrimp Louie, Combination Seafood Platter, Halibut Florentine, Veal Piccata (you can also have both the halibut and veal), and Baked Salmon Wellington. Another favorite is the Lobster-Fillet combination.

SANTA BARBARA

Harbor Restaurant

210 Stearns Wharf
Santa Barbara
California
Telephone: 805–963–3311

All major credit cards
Lunch and dinner
Reservations not necessary
Jacket required only in Santa Barbara Room
Liquor served
Dinner: $8.95 to $20
full 3 courses, without wine
Lunch: $4.95 to $12
Chef: Kevin Sherry

Some feel that the view of old Stearns Wharf from the Harbor Restaurant is as delightful as the view from Stearn's Wharf itself. The wharf looks like a tiny New England fishing village mounted on a long pier, and, set against a background of palm trees and bright blue water, it is very picturesque.

Stearns Wharf has been around since 1872, when John P. Stearns, financed by a Santa Barbara millionaire, Colonel William Welles Hollister, got the city council to give its blessings for the construction of a town wharf. It has had many owners, including the Coast Guard (during World War II) and actor James Cagney, and it often suffered from physical neglect. Today the wharf is operated by the city of Santa Barbara and has, in addition to the luxurious Harbor Restaurant, an enclave of shops and other restaurants in rustic seaside-style buildings.

Like the wharf, the Harbor Restaurant has had a checkered history since its inception in 1941. It was first opened in what had been the Santa Barbara Yacht Club's old wharf-end clubhouse. In 1963, it was refurbished and became a successful showplace, only to be destroyed by a fire in 1973. Rebuilt, the new Harbor Restaurant manages to capture the decor and spirit of its three-decade history. It offers extensive lunch and dinner menus, featuring what it proclaims to be a "seafood menu unmatched on the Pacific coast, and is enhanced with pasta made fresh daily in the grand style of Northern Italy."

Popular with local residents, it is also a favorite of tourists in the area.

UNIVERSAL CITY

Oscars at the Premiere

Sheraton at Universal City
555 Universal Terrace
Universal City
California 91608
Telephone: 818–506–2500

All major credit cards
Lunch and dinner
Reservations necessary
Jacket required
Liquor served
Dinner: $17 to $26
full 3 courses, without wine
Lunch: $12 to $27
Chef: Tim Knowlton
Maitre d': Bill Simmons

How would you like a view to dine by in Hollywood? Well, this is the most elegant one to be had.

Oscars at the Premiere, the signature dining room of the Sheraton Premiere Hotel, is a luxury dining room providing a formal yet intimate setting. Right next door to the Universal Studios, this 24-story glass hotel tower, designed by famed architect William Pereira, overlooks Hollywood and the San Fernando Valley. The tower contains 450 guest rooms and has 19 suites on its top five floors, including two 2,400 square foot presidential suites—bona fide Hollywood opulence. The restaurants of the hotel and meeting places are in three 40-floor high pavilions, also mostly glass enclosed, adjoining the residential tower.

The smallest full dining room in this hotel is the extravagant and elegant Oscars at the Premiere, named for the award many of its guests strive to earn. It seats 80 people.

Oscars at the Premiere

Chef Timothy A. Knowlton features fabulous foods of the newly rediscovered American cuisine, which is rapidly becoming a national favorite. The menu includes such items as New Orleans-style Blackened Tenderloin and Smoked Scallops with Raspberry Vinegar.

Opened in April, this extraordinary dining room is a delight for the eye. Its decor features antique mirrors, elaborate crystal chandeliers and flower arrangements, and a coffered ceiling. There is a central banquette as well as large individual tables with beautiful wood-framed, brocade-covered chairs. Sparkling Villeroy and Boch crystal, Mintin and Royal Doulton porcelain china, and richly designed Reed and Barton silver allows each table to be a study in elegance.

In keeping with the level of the decor and the settings, the ceremony of guest service is genteel as well. The menu is presented in a large white envelope, addressed with each guest's name.

It is a long and varied menu, so time is needed just to read it, let alone make a decision. To avert painful hunger pangs, guests are treated to complimentary chicken liver pâté served with toasted French bread. The pâté is very light and silky in texture because it has been blended with port and cream. Guests here are encouraged to forget restraint and order everything that looks good. Unfortunately, everything looks good!

Among the appetizer delights, for example, are a New Orleans-style skillet-fried Shrimp in Spicy Butter and Glazed Lobster with a sauce of puréed fresh chives and white wine.

Salad choices include red leaf lettuce pieces tossed with toasted pine nuts, wisps of carrots, red peppers, and smoked-on-the-premises duck in a honey-fresh lime dressing, or the endive salad with warmed goat's cheese tossed with walnut oil vinaigrette.

The main dishes are all special. It seems an effort is made to make the usual unusual. There is, for example, the usual prime rib, but it is roasted in a smoker. Other entrées include tender chunks of lobster smothered in a richly flavored reduction of crayfish stock, cream, brandy, and tarragon. Placed in the center of the lobster plate is a mound of fresh pasta made with Pinot Noir wine.

If you have room for dessert, you'll have a problem in deciding, of course. Oscars' fresh fruit soufflés are the favorites here. Blueberry and raspberry are featured.

This dining room is open Monday through Friday for lunch from 11:30 A.M. to 2 P.M., and for dinner Monday through Saturday from 6 P.M. until 10 P.M.

COLORADO
DENVER

Augusta
The Westin Hotel
Tabor Center Denver
1672 Lawrence Street
Denver
Colorado 80202
Telephone: 303–572–9100

All major credit cards
Lunch and dinner
Reservations recommended
Jacket and tie preferred
Liquor served
Dinner: $20 to $30
     full 3 courses, without wine
Lunch: $10 to $13
Chef: Serge Delage
Maitre d': James Twiford

The Augusta is a dining room featuring American cuisine, located directly off the lobby of the Westin Hotel, with which it shares a view of Denver's downtown skyline and Skyline Park. The dining room itself is very dramatic, with its background of padded gray satin walls showing off the polished brass and etched glass panels, ebony-lacquered furnishings, and peach-colored upholstery. The design is reminiscent of Art Deco.

The American cuisine features dishes either from the rotisserie or ones that are grilled, broiled, or steamed. The food is always light and sometimes consists of unique and exciting, or at least interesting, combinations. Among the favorites are duck and chicken prepared on the rotisserie. Local critics have rated Augusta among the best dining rooms in the city.

Desserts include a rich and sinful Chocolate Mousse, rich fancy cakes, and our favorite, Bread Pudding with Whiskey Sauce.

The hotel is situated in Tabor Center, which contains the 420-room Westin Hotel, a collection of 70 shops and eateries, and a 32-story office tower. It is named for Horace Tabor, an early pioneer developer in Colorado. The Augusta restaurant is named for the first wife of this legendary figure.

EL RANCHO

El Rancho Colorado

18 Miles West of Denver on I-70
El Ranch Exit #252
Denver/El Rancho
Colorado 80401
Telephone: 303–526–0661

All major credit cards
Lunch, dinner, and Sunday brunch
Reservations not required
Dress: casual
Liquor served
Dinner: $10 to $20
     full 3 courses, without wine
Lunch: $5 to $11
Owner: Paul R. McEncroe

El Rancho Colorado, at 7,686 feet above sea level, is a great mountain dining lodge that offers what many writers claim is one of the most photographed views in Colorado and, some say, in America as well. It is indeed spectacular—the snowcapped Continental Divide of the Rocky Mountains rises dramatically in the distance.

The restaurant here has seven fireplaces, and has been expanded over the years. Back in 1954 72 guests could be seated. Today the seating capacity has increased to 225 in three mid-level areas, and in three lower-level dining rooms there's room for 125 more. All this additional seating has been provided without spoiling the elegant atmosphere.

Lunch is served from 11:30 A.M. until 2 P.M., dinner from 5 P.M. to 10 P.M., Sunday brunch from 9:30 A.M. until 1:30 P.M., and Sunday dinner from 2 P.M. until 8:30 P.M. Among the main dish specialties are Australia Rock Lobster Tail, Filet Mignon Rock Lobster Tail, Beef El Rancho, New York Strip Sirloin Steak, and Fresh Mountain Trout. A great favorite here (which you can also buy and take with you) are the delicious home-baked cinnamon rolls. The dessert selections are different and exciting every day.

Best time to dine with a view is just before sunset.

VAIL

Wildflower Inn at the Lodge at Vail

174 East Gore Creek Drive
Vail
Colorado 81657
Telephone: 303–476–5011

All major credit cards
Dinner
Reservations recommended
Jacket and tie required
Liquor served
Dinner: $25 to $35
full 3 courses, without wine
Chef: Jim Cohen

At the magnificently refurbished Lodge at Vail, in the heart of Vail Village, there is a delightful new gourmet restaurant called the Wildflower Inn. It is so beautiful that it won the first-place award for its interior design for 1985 from the restaurant industry publication, *Restaurant Hospitality.*

The prize-winning interior was created by Warren Platner of New Haven, Connecticut, known for having designed New York's Windows on the World Restaurant at the World Trade Center (also discussed in this book). The theme of the decor is that of a spring garden in bloom, giving the restaurant an overall atmosphere of warmth, elegance, and charm. Huge baskets of colorful silk flowers were personally arranged by Mr. Platner. The tables are richly set with Villeroy and Boch China, Reed and Barton silver, Zwiesel crystal, and Laura Ashley table linens.

The view from the Wildflower Inn is spectacular: the Rocky Mountains, covered with wildflowers during the spring and summer, snow-capped peaks glistening in the sun, or submerged under layers of crystalline snow in winter.

The superb cuisine served by Chef Cohen features a small but diverse menu whose specialties include Fresh Tuna Steak prepared in a peppery Tuscany oil, Rack of Lamb covered with Pine Nuts, Garlic, and Jalapeño Peppers, Breast of Pheasant, Lamb Loin, and Veal Chop Sauté.

CONNECTICUT

STAMFORD

The Swan Court

The Inn at Mill River
26 Mill River Road
Stamford
Connecticut 06902
Telephone: 203–325–1900

All major credit cards
Breakfast, lunch, and dinner
Reservations necessary
Jacket required at dinner
Liquor served
Dinner: $30 to $45
full 3 courses, without wine
Lunch: $15 to $30
Chef: Maxime Ribera
Maitre d': John Zerega

One of the most elegant restaurants in Stamford, indeed in all of Connecticut, the Swan Court was awarded three stars by the food critic of the *New York Times.*

The Inn at Mill River is a favorite of the more affluent business people in Stamford, which is home to many national corporations' headquarters. The Swan Court Restaurant has windows overlooking a Japanese cherry tree promenade along the Mill River, which winds through the city limits and empties into Long Island Sound. While it is most delightful here at cherry blossom time in the spring, this restaurant affords a pleasant and tranquil view any time of the year.

The dining room is beautifully decorated, with latticed walls in peach and cream tones and Oriental touches such as blue and white vases and other decorative objects. The skirted tables are beautifully set with fine Wedgwood porcelain and handblown crystal. The authentic French cuisine is enhanced by the finest of local ingredients. The food is prepared on the premises with the expertise and original recipes of the Inn's well-known culinary advisers, including the French chefs Jean-Michel Gammariello and Jean-Pierre Vuillermet, and Clive Ranfay, an English pastry expert.

The menu is excellent. For starters you can have Tuna and Swordfish, a Three-Vegetable Mousse, or a savory Sauté of Artichoke Hearts in an orange-sparked Provencal sauce. All are presented as colorful and artistic masterpieces which look as grand as they taste.

Among the popular main dishes are Grilled Half Cornish Hen, Baked Monkfish, Breast of Long Island Duckling, and Sliced Medallions of Veal.

All of the desserts are fantastic. Among them are a tantalizing deep dark Chocolate Mousse in a toasted almond brioche crust, floating in vanilla sauce with toasted almonds; warm Almond Tart, composed of pear, almond cream, and caramelized pear sauce; Tart Nougatine with three homemade sorbets—black currant, raspberry, and passion fruit, neatly packaged in a crisp pecan-caramel box; homemade Pistachio Ice Cream in Sabayon; Mill River Mosaic of Three Ice Creams; and Chocolate Plaisir, a velvet-rich dark and white chocolate mousse, with a topping of pastry and chocolate sauce. Had enough?

Sunday brunch is available, too, from 11 A.M. until 2 P.M., for a reasonable $7 to $15 for entrées.

WESTON

Cobbs Mill Inn by the Waterfall

Old Mill Road	*All major credit cards*
Route 57	*Dinner*
Weston	*Reservations preferred*
Connecticut 06883	*Jacket recommended*
Telephone: 203–227–7221	*Liquor served*
	Dinner: $14.75
	full two courses, without wine and dessert
	Proprietor: Julie P. Jones

In one of the oldest structures in the country, you can enjoy dinner with a view of a forty-feet-high waterfall formed as a small part of the Saugatuck River passes over a two hundred year old dam. Cobbs Mill Inn sits at the edge of a pond that is home to a number of ducks, adding to the quaint scene. The Inn itself was built between 1750 and 1775, predating the Revolutionary War, so you get to absorb some New England history as you dine. It sits within a Colonial style garden, attractively interrupted by outcroppings of rugged rock. The view can be enjoyed from the dining room at the top of the falls, or from the cocktail lounge, a floor below, at the foot of the falls.

The cuisine is American, featuring fresh foods of the season, all attractively prepared and pleasantly served.

FLORIDA
BAL HARBOUR

Coco's Sidewalk Café

9700 Collins Avenue
Bal Harbour
Florida 33154
Telephone: 305-864-2626

All major credit cards
Breakfast, lunch, and dinner
Reservations not required
Dress: casual
Liquor served
Dinner: $15.95
   full 3 courses, without wine
Lunch: $5.95
Owner: David Migicovsky
Maitre d': Lori Migicovsky

People-watching, particularly if these people are fashionable shoppers in a chic area, can be an entertaining experience. Coco's offers just such enjoyment, whether you're there for breakfast, twilight dinner, or the happy hour that takes place some time in between. And if that sort of entertainment isn't enough for you, some other type of diversion is always provided—a pianist, an accordionist, sometimes even a palmist.

Casual elegance is the catch phrase here. The waiters are all dressed as if they stepped out of the pages of a fashion magazine, and all are skilled in the art of food presentation, as part of a show put on by the proprietor, David Migicovsky.

When David came here from Montreal his objective was to achieve a Continental and cosmopolitan setting, and he decided that an outdoor café was the way to do it. He was the first to bring this style of dining to Florida.

Inasmuch as his customers were the stylish ladies who shop in the chic Bal Harbour stores, he elected to have a fashion theme for the restaurant's decor. Coco's was named for Coco Chanel, considered by David to be the first designer to "liberate women's fashions."

The style of the cuisine is called American, but it is a bit different because of the special Continental touches added by David. Salads, such as the famous Nicoise, are served in glass flowerpots. Specialties include homemade Lasagne, gourmet burgers, pita sandwiches, Asparagus Parmesan, and Cajun-style fish and steak.

Some of the favorite desserts include frozen Key Lime Pie, Oreo Biscuit Cheesecake, warm Apple Dumpling with Cinnamon Ice Cream and Caramel Sauce, Apple Pie with French Vanilla Ice Cream and Caramel Sauce, Pecan Pie, and Chocolate Kiss—a thick chocolate brownie topped with caramel ice cream and drizzled with coffee syrup.

In keeping with the chic location, this is one of the few spots in Miami where a guest can take her poodle to lunch and have him/her served out of a personalized water dish. Really.

BAY HARBOR ISLAND

Café Chauveron

9561 East Bay Harbor Drive
Bay Harbor Island
Florida
Telephone: 305-866-8779

All major credit cards
Dinner
Reservations necessary
Jacket required
Liquor served
Dinner: $45
   full 3 courses, without wine
Chef: Terry Left
Maitre d': Jean Claude Troadec

If you've wondered what happened to a wonderful New York restaurant called Chauveron, now you know: it's in Florida.

The late Roger Chauveron, restaurateur extraordinaire, opened the Chambord in New York City in 1935; it became one of the foremost restaurants in the nation. In 1957, he followed that achievement with another—Café Chauveron. It, too, was an immediate success, attracting the rich and the famous.

When Café Chauveron lost its least to Citicorp, Roger decided to move the restaurant to Miami, opening the Bay Harbor Island restaurant under the same name at the end of 1972. André Chauveron, who began learning the restaurant business in his dad's kitchen when he was only 17, became a partner in the enterprise and by October 1984 had taken over as the owner/host.

Apparently André has done a good job. The restaurant recently received the prestigious *Mobil Travel Guide* Five-Star Award for the 11th consecutive year. The *Miami Herald* restaurant critic awarded Café Chauveron top honors with four stars, the highest amount possible.

On a menu offering *"La Cuisine Francaise pour les Gourmets,"* these are the most popular items: Imported Dover Sole *Bonne Femme ou Sautée ou Grillee,* Red Snapper *Roti Beurre Blanc* and Fennel, *Les Belles Cailles Roties en Cocotte Flambees au Cognac* (when game is in season), and *Le Roi Faisan a la Mode du Maitre Perigourdin.*

The favorites among a lengthy list of tempting desserts are the *Mousse au Chocolate du Chef* with Sabayon Sauce and the three different soufflés—Chauveron, Grand Marnier, or Chocolate. These must be ordered at the beginning of the meal.

The restaurant itself is not as beautiful as the commanding view of the bay from its main dining room. The terraced dining room has a bar on a higher level; the dining tables here also have a nice view. André is spending time and money in beautifying the restaurant; in 1986 the color scheme will be changed to French blue with touches of apricot and the chairs will be replaced with ones in French Provincial style.

André is proud of the prestige his father achieved with his restaurants in New York and with Café Chauveron here in Florida. When his father died a few years ago, André was determined to keep up the standards that won this restaurant so many honors. Only Lutèce in New York, Ernie's in San Francisco, and La Maisonette in Cincinnati have received the *Mobil* guide's Five-Star Award more times than Café Chauveron.

One of André's fondest stories is about a couple who recently celebrated a wedding anniversary in his restaurant. They had first visited Café Chauveron in New York in 1962 and told André that nothing had changed, that everything was now as they recalled it had been in 1962. That, to André, is even more reassuring than a critic's stars.

FORT LAUDERDALE

Le Dome of The Four Seasons

333 Sunset Drive
Fort Lauderdale
Florida 33301
Telephone: 305-463-3303

All major credit cards
Dinner at 6 P.M. only
Reservations required
Jacket required
Liquor served
Dinner: $14 to $35
full 3 courses, without wine
Chef: Alain "Vincent" Barrere
Maitre d'/Proprietor: John Carlone

This penthouse restaurant, opened since January 1964, is one of the most elegant and distinguished in Florida. Situated atop the Four Seasons apartment building, which was purchased by Calvin Houghland in 1962, Le Dome is the product of one man's vision. Houghland, of Nashville, Tennessee and Fort Lauderdale, is a businessman, rancher, and international sportsman who likes the best. With an eye toward opening a restaurant of his own, he conducted a survey of the great restaurants of Europe; after a year and a half spent analyzing the results, planning, construction, and decoration, Le Dome was opened.

The view from the top of the condominium building is a panorama of Fort Lauderdale, the Intercoastal Waterway which flows by the building at its base, and the Atlantic Ocean. The food is also a highlight—Le Dome continues to receive honors and awards for what it calls "California Nouvelle Cuisine," among them the Golden Spoon Award and Four Stars from the *Mobil* guide.

The tasteful decor is by one of the country's leading designers, Wells M. Squier, of Fort Lauderdale. Most attractive is the enhancement of the interior by the display of original art. Five of the oil paintings are by Mrs. Houghland; others are contributions from the French artist Jean George Vibert from the Jay Gould collection; Gerard Ellis, who painted for the royal family of England; B. Delaroche, another French artist; Robert Curran Smith, of Orlando, Florida; and Jolie Gabor, mother of Zsa Zsa and Eva.

LAKE WALES

Chalet Suzanne Restaurant
and Country Inn

P.O. Drawer AC
US Route 27 and 17A
Lake Wales
Florida 33859–9003
Telephone: 813–676–6011

All major credit cards
Breakfast, lunch, and dinner
Reservations preferred
Jacket preferred
Liquor served
Dinner: $33 to $43
    6 courses, without wine
Lunch: $18 to $26
Chef: Carl Hinshaw
Hostess: Vita Hinshaw

This is a magnificent and imaginative hodgepodge of architecture housing an exuberant place to eat. You first realize you have a unique experience in store for you when you see the driveway to the inn, which meanders through orange groves leading to the restaurant on the edge of Lake Suzanne. You can't believe what you see! Turret-topped and rambling, this complex of buildings is painted in various pastels and features a mosaic-bordered pool, a French patio overlooking it, and much decorative wrought iron. There is also a 2,450-feet-long air strip nearby. Why so much variety? Simple—the Hinshaw family likes to feel that this inn reflects the diversity of the world at large.

The dining room is a delight, not only with its antiques, stained glass, and old lamps, but in its unique setting of quaint rooms on many levels. Just as no two rooms are alike, no two tables are set alike. Dinner is by candlelight, and fresh flowers are on every table.

The cuisine has been saluted with four stars from the *Mobil* guide and a Golden Spoon Award. Among the dishes featured are Broiled Grapefruit, Soup Romaine, Chicken Suzanne, Lobster Newburg, Shrimp Curry, Lump Crab, Shad Roe, Lamb Chop Grill, Filet Mignon, and, for dessert, *Gateau Christina*. This is down to earth, good, and substantial food.

MIAMI

The Cove

Miami Airport Hilton and Marina
5101 Blue Lagoon Drive
Miami
Florida 33126
Telephone: 305–262–1000 Ext. 67

All major credit cards
Lunch and dinner
Reservations required
Jacket not required
Liquor served
Dinner: $13.95 to $21.95
    full 3 courses, without wine
Lunch: $4.95 to $8.95
Chef: Stephen Sappe
Maitre d': Bruce Ahart

The Cove

The Cove dining room at this airport/marina hotel has two views to delight its guests: interior and exterior. In fact, the view created within the dining room has received national recognition—the Cove was awarded the 1984 Designer Circle Award from *Lodging and Hospitality* magazine and the 1984 Table Top Award.

The decor of the dining room blends grays with real blues, accented by shades of shrimp. These colors form the muted backdrop for the Cove's featured item—a striking 1,000 gallon aquarium containing brightly colored tropical fish living in coral water. A large pastel painting in a single acrylic frame dramatically reinforces the ocean theme.

The exterior view complements the decor. Tiered levels within the dining room offer guests at every table breathtaking views of the Blue Lagoon: a delightful view to dine by.

The cuisine features some of Florida's most popular seafood, from Florida lobster and stone crabs to the more delicate flavors of pompano and swordfish. For the landlubber, Veal Princess and *Tournedos* Lichtenstein are on the menu. Other popular main dishes include Pompano *Francaise,* Minted Shrimp, and Scallops *Ticconese.*

Highlighting the spectacular dessert display are two favorites—Macadamia Pie and Chocolate Rum Cake. There is a new wine bar in the dining room.

MIAMI BEACH

Dominique's Restaurant

Alexander Hotel
5225 Collins Avenue
Miami Beach
Florida 33140
Telephone: 305–865–6500

All major credit cards
Lunch and dinner
Reservations suggested
Jacket requested
Liquor served
Dinner: $25 to $50
    full 3 courses, without wine
Owner: Dominique D'Ermo
Food and Beverage Director: Henry Sillman

Dominique's famous French restaurant at the Alexander Hotel on Miami Beach shares the name of its sister restaurant in Washington, D.C., long regarded as one of the capital city's best. The elegant main dining room in the Florida restaurant, filled with antiques and original artwork, overlooks the Atlantic Ocean and the lush gardens of the Alexander Hotel.

Dominique's

The restaurant is well appointed inside as well. From the sumptuous Renaissance Lounge on the mezzanine level, a glassed-in promenade walkway winds through tropical gardens, past a pair of antique brass gates and other treasures, ending at a striking marble foyer framed by intricate stained and beveled glass panels and a finely carved Victorian bench with ormolu embellishment.

To the left is Dominique's Lounge, an intimate spot for before- or after-dinner cocktails. To the right is the elegant main dining room, with bay windows overlooking a bubbling fountain and a meandering brook leading to cascades that tumble over coral grottoes into two lagoon swimming pools. Immediately beyond is a wide expanse of white sand beach and the Atlantic Ocean.

The decor blends soft tones of pink, deep burgundy, Hunter green, and beiges to complement the Alexander's lush tropical landscaping, creating a pleasant backdrop for Dominique's exquisite antique furnishings. Among the treasures in the dining room are an ornate clock, a lion sculpture, columns with a fruit motif carved in England (circa 1870), a turn-of-the-century piano with burled and inlaid wood detailing, and intricate coffered paneling. Smoked mirrors create a *faux* balcony effect on three sides of the dining room, accentuated by provincial open chandeliers. Original oil paintings cover the walls; Oriental carpets are on the parquet floor.

The cuisine is also a major attraction. To ensure its reputation for freshness and quality, Dominique's flies in much of its produce and game directly from Dominique D'Ermo's estate on the eastern Shore of Maryland.

Dominique's fare often tends toward the exotic. Among the current unusual seasonal offerings are Buffalo Sausages, Diamondback Rattlesnake Salad, and Alligator Tail, all served as dinner appetizers. Those with less adventurous appetites shouldn't worry about finding enough on the menu to satisfy; Dominique's has exquisite conventional fare as well.

First course choices include *Quail Pâté en Brioche* with Raspberry Sauce, Shrimp with Ginger Sauce, and U.S. Senate Dining Room Bean Soup. Entrées include Grilled Salmon with Watercress and Dill Sauce (the house specialty), Marinated Rack of Lamb, prime New York Sirloin Steak stuffed with Escargots and Garlic Butter, and Veal Scallopini.

The desserts are a sight to behold. The Blackout Cake is at least six inches high, adorned with a thick, rich chocolate butter cream. Another tempting dessert, which combines chocolate-dribbled whipped cream with chocolate truffles, is named in honor of Farrah Fawcett and Elizabeth Taylor.

ORLANDO

Atlantis
Wyndham Hotel Sea World
6677 Sea Harbor Drive
Orlando
Florida 32821
Telephone: 305-351-5555

All major credit cards
Dinner
Reservations required
Jacket required
Liquor served
Dinner: $25 to $45
    full 3 courses, without wine
Chef: Michel Paton
Maitre d': Ralph Rendsland

The Atlantis Restaurant, the gourmet restaurant for Wyndham Hotel Sea World, is a pleasant surprise. Located just off the spectacular 65,000 square foot atrium/lobby—said to be the world's largest—of the new luxurious Wyndham Hotel Sea World in Orlando, the Atlantis offers the ultimate in elegance and has drawn rave reviews for its French nouvelle cuisine ever since the hotel and restaurant opened in December 1984.

At Atlantis the diners sit amid a lush decor of rich wood paneling, crystal chandeliers, fine European oil paintings, and warm-colored walls and furniture. A touch of Florida is provided by three large ceiling murals with tropical themes, painted by Dallas artist William A. Foley. Outside the restaurant is an astounding view—the hotel's spectacular atrium and lobby, which combined is longer and wider than a football field and features soaring palms, lush tropical foliage, a variety of shops, exotic Japanese Koi fish swimming in a large pond, and waterfall-filled pools.

The food is splendid and well-presented. Everything starts with a small portion of an *amusegueule,* which translated means "a bit of something to amuse the mouth." It might be, for example, Scallop Mousse with Oysters and Mussels in a suave sauce.

Other starters include Lobster and Truffle Bisque, Avocado Mousse with CrabMeat, and Assorted Leaf Lettuces adorned with goat cheese on tender toast points.

Some of the fine main dishes are Sliced Breast of Duck with Wine Sauce and Mango, Medallions of Spring Lamb, and Red Snapper Wrapped in Romaine Lettuce. Most expensive and delightful is the Lobster Mousse in Ravioli with Sliced Lobster Tail and Truffles.

The desserts are a threat to any diet and present a tough choice. Here are just a few of the favorites: Dacquoise Cake, Chocolate Mousse Cake, Bavarian Cream Cake topped with pears, and Raspberry Sauce over Strawberry and Almond Pastry—great!

Atlantis maitre d' Rendsland tells of the time that Bob Hope entered the gourmet dining room through the kitchen because of security reasons, much to the delight of the staff members, who gave him such a warm and enthusiastic greeting that Hope autographed everyone's chef's hat before going into the dining room.

Haifeng Restaurant

Wyndham Hotel Sea World
6677 Sea Harbor Drive
Orlando
Florida 32821
Telephone: 305–351–5555

All major credit cards
Dinner
Reservations necessary
Jacket requested
Liquor served
Chef: Danny Chu
Maitre d': Philip Yu

Like the Atlantis, this restaurant is located off the immense Wyndham Hotel Sea World lobby. Haifeng serves imaginatively prepared oriental food in a sophisticated setting.

The restaurant is uniquely decorated in neutral shades of gray and black to help set off the subtle yet powerful water color paintings on rice paper by the Chinese artist Li Shan, whose work also hangs in the Great Hall of the People in Peking.

A large glass window separating the restaurant from the kitchen provides an interesting view to dine by, that of the chefs at work.

A popular dining place, Haifeng's celebrity guests have included Bob Hope, Winnie Palmer (wife of the golfing great Arnold Palmer), actress Beverly Garland, a recent Miss Florida, and others.

PORT ST. LUCIE

The Brass Sandpiper Restaurant

The Sandpiper Bay Resort Hotel & Marina
Port St. Lucie
Florida 33452
Telephone: 305–335–4400

All major credit cards
Breakfast, lunch, dinner, and Sunday brunch
Reservations requested
Jacket requested
Liquor served
Dinner: $17 to $25
*   full 3 courses, without wine*
Lunch: $8 to $12
Chef: Francois Peter
Maitre d': Allan Davis

The beautiful Brass Sandpiper Restaurant of the Sandpiper Bay Resort Hotel and Marina offers its guests luxurious dining in a room with massive wooden beams, a cathedral ceiling, a fine tapestry, and best of all, picture windows overlooking the waters of the mile-wide St. Lucie River.

This is the restaurant of a luxury resort, and as such it features an international cuisine, a daily change of menu, a choice of a dozen hot and cold appetizers, the freshest seafood, prime aged meats, crisp salads, vegetables—and, for dessert, scrumptuous soufflés.

Friday night a bountiful seafood buffet is featured, and on Sunday the brunch is generous and picturesque.

Among the favorites on the menu are the Mesquite-Grilled Fish as a main course, and, as desserts, Key Lime Pie and Mud Pie.

The cuisine won the 1985 Silver Spoon Award from the Gourmet Diners Club of America.

Port St. Lucie is an hour from the Palm Beach International Airport and two hours north of Miami. To reach Sandpiper Bay, take exit 54 at Port St. Lucie off the Florida Turnpike.

HAWAII
HONOLULU

La Mer

Halekulani Hotel
2199 Kalia Road
Honolulu
Hawaii 96815
Telephone: 808–923–2311

All major credit cards
Dinner and Sunday brunch
Reservations necessary
Jacket required
Liquor served
Dinner: $40 to $65
*   full 3 courses, without wine*
Chef: Khamtan Tanhchaleun
Maitre d': Michael Flickinger

La Mer at the Halekulani Hotel ranks among Hawaii's finest restaurant; in fact, a recent review in the *Wall Street Journal* said that it is generally regarded by food experts as the best in Honolulu. That's saying a lot, for there are a number of very good restaurants in Honolulu and nearby Waikiki.

Creative French cuisine is offered nightly, along with spectacular views of the sea of Waikiki and the famous trademark of the area, Diamond Head rock.

The menus change weekly, with specialties including Fresh Duck Liver pâté, Island fish, and a spectacular strawberry dessert. Many of these dishes are the creations of consulting chef Philippe Chavent from Lyon, France, who visits La Mer at least three times a year. In exchange, Chef Tanhchaleun, in late 1985, went to Lyon for three weeks to work and observe in Philippe's La Tour Rose.

Meals are elegant here. A selection of items, from start to finish, will give you the picture: for appetizers, there are Prawn Bisque with Saffron and Scallions, Fresh Duck Liver Terrino, and Warm Spinach Salad with Sesame Prawns. Medallions of Lobster with Asparagus and Lobster Sauce, Sautéed Moana with Curry Sauce, Sautéed Makinnah Steak with Ginger and Lime Sauce, Beef Tenderloin with Sweet Bell Pepper Sauce, Breast of Duck with Green Peppercorn Sauce, and Medallions of Veal with Garlic Sauce and Snow Peas are just a few of the entrées. For dessert try a Strawberry Sunburst or Chocolate Mousse Cake—or pastries and fruits from the dessert cart.

The Willows

901 Hausten Street
Honolulu
Hawaii 96826
Telephone: 808-946-4808

All major credit cards
Lunch and dinner
Reservation suggested, particularly
  for the Kamaaina Suite
Dress: casual, but neat
Dinner: $15 to $35
  full 3 courses, without wine
Lunch: the same
Executive chef: Kusuma Cooray

The Willows is one of Hawaii's oldest and most popular restaurants; located in Moiiliili, a short ride from Waikiki, it has been in operation for more than forty years. The restaurant is made up of thatched cabanas which surround the main attraction—the koi-filled ponds where the *alii* (royalty) came to bathe. Tropical gardens add a wonderful touch.

The Willows offers award-winning cuisine, the preparation of which is supervised by Cordon Bleu-trained executive chef Cooray, a native of Sri Lanka. The cuisine blends the finest Eastern and Western ingredients.

Our favorite room to dine in is the Kamaaina Suite, a quiet, private dining room on the second floor of a building in the gardens overlooking the ponds. It has only a few tables and its special price-fixed menu is truly the *pièce de resistance* of the entire place.

Whether at dinner or brunch, the strolling musicians at the Willows are most entertaining. Lunchtime is very popular here, especially on Thursdays when an event called "Poi Thursday" is hosted by Auntie Irmgard Aluli and her Puama Trio. The show features dancers and singers and guests are invited to join in.

There are so many popular items on the menu that it is difficult to select just a few.

But some favorites include Sri Lankan Curry, using Chef Cooray's personal recipe, prepared with either fresh island chicken or shrimp; traditional Hawaiian Curry, rich with coconut cream and made with a choice of chicken, shrimp, or fresh vegetables; and Pacific Salmon, enhanced with a delicate seafood mousseline and an herb *beurre blanc.*

Among the appetizers, Chef Cooray's signature Spinach Timbale (a light spinach mousse topped with cheese sauce), *Lomi* Salmon and *Poi* (a Hawaiian favorite), and Angel Hair Pasta with prosciutto ham are fine choices.

The dessert menu at the Willows is a real challenge. One favorite is the coconut or lemon Sky High Pie with many inches of meringue. Another is Chef Cooray's chocolate *Gateau,* topped with chantilly cream—truly one of the world's best chocolate cakes! There are special desserts on holidays. At Thanksgiving, for example, you can order Pink Chiffon Pumpkin Pie with meringue!

Other desserts to ponder are Chocolate-*Haupia* Cake (dream cake with a layer of Hawaiian coconut pudding and a creamy mocha filling), Sinless Cheesecake, A Thing of Beauty (a deep chocolate confection in a macadamia-graham crust), Black Forest Crêpes (vanilla ice cream in homemade crepes topped with hot Bing cherries, whipped cream, and grated chocolate), and Sunny Lee's Guava Glue Sundae (a light fresh guava purée over macadamia nut ice cream). The *Nawiliwli* and *Keoki* coffees are very special, too.

The cuisine here has won the *Travel/Holiday* Magazine Award and the Golden Fork Award from the International Society of Food, Travel, and Wine Writers. *Gourmet* magazine has featured its Hawaiian food recipes. The *Poi* suppers and lunches offer local people and visitors a chance to sample native cuisine including *laulau,* sweet potato, chicken luau, *pipi kaula, lomi* salmon, fresh *poi, limu kohu,* Hawaiian rock salt, green onion, fresh pineapple, and *haupia.*

Windows of Hawaii

1441 Kapiolani Boulevard
Honolulu
Hawaii 96814
Telephone: 808-941-9138

All major credit cards
Breakfast, lunch, dinner,
* and late supper*
Reservations recommended
Jacket not required
Liquor served
Dinner: $9 to $24
* full 3 courses, without wine*
Lunch: $6 to $12
Chef: James Craig
Maitre d': Rory Horning

Twenty-five years ago, when this restaurant was opened under the name of La Ronde, it was the first revolving restaurant in America. It was a unique delight for visitors to Hawaii, for while dining they were able to see all of Honolulu and Waikiki.

Both the restaurant and the view have changed considerably. The restaurant is now called Windows of Hawaii and has just opened after being completely refurbished. Gone are the old, worn, cumbersome, space-consuming brown naugahyde dining booths that partially blocked the beautiful view, and the dull, drab, dark brown walls are now covered with a colorful Wyland mural called *Dolphin Heaven* which depicts dolphins and other beautiful sea creatures from the Hawaiian waters, some of which (not the dolphins!) are served at the restaurant.

The view is also better than ever because you can see more of it more easily. Located atop a building in one of the world's largest shopping centers, the restaurant offers a full view of the mountains, the Ala Wai boat harbor, the Ala Moana Beach Park, downtown Honolulu, and Waikiki, all dominated by Diamond Head. There are more skyscraper hotels and office buildings to see, but much to our surprise, these do not destroy the beauty of the view.

The food has improved, too. There's good reason: Windows of Hawaii's fish buyer has been buying fish for a long time and he personally knows the operators of all the major fishing boats working out of the island of Oahu. The restaurant has a perfect view of the sea and the harbors so the fish buyer can make sightings to determine when the fishing ships are coming in.

Lunch is popular at Windows on Hawaii because of a novel presentation called the "seawich" (which could just as easily be named the "crabwich," since it has a liberal offering of crab), which is served with the pleasant locally grown Manoa lettuce and slices of tasty wine-ripened tomato. The other sandwiches include roast beef, steak, sweet ham, chicken salad, tuna, and fresh fish. Lunch is served Monday through Friday from 11 A.M. until 2 P.M.

Dinner is our favorite time here. The spectacular sunsets turn the sky into a patchwork quilt of oranges, pinks, and magentas. And later you see the silvery glow of the moon on the tranquil ocean. Dinner offers a choice of appetizers such as shrimp and crableg cocktails, fettucine, sashimi, or escargots. The soups are special, including a zesty Portuguese bean soup, Queen's Seafood Chowder, or the favorite—Chef James' French Onion Soup. Among the classic entrée choices are Roast Prime Rib of Beef, Chateaubriand, Steak Kabobs, or Tarragon Veal Scaloppine. The fish is fresh and the meats are cut each day. There is also a choice of New England cuisine. Only fresh vegetables are served. Dinner is served from 5 P.M. until 10 P.M. On Saturdays and Sundays from 10 A.M. until 2 P.M. a continuous champagne and wine buffet is served. On Thursdays, Fridays, and Saturdays from 10 P.M. until midnight, moonlight suppers are served for the after-show people.

About half the patrons of Windows on Hawaii are tourists; the rest are local people. You can park just below the restaurant, or if it is easier, just take a number eight bus from any place in Waikiki and you'll be let off nearby.

Windows of Hawaii holds 350 people and is over 400 feet high, revolving 360 degrees each hour, at a rate of 3.5 feet per minute.

MAUI

Swan Court

Hyatt Regency Maui
200 Nohea Kai Drive
Lahaina, Maui
Hawaii 96761
Telephone: 808–667–7474

All major credit cards
Breakfast and dinner
Reservations necessary
Jacket not required
Liquor served
Dinner: $18 to $28
   full 3 courses, without wine
Chef: Harry Gabel
Maitre d': Ed Brea

Imagine selecting one of the most beautiful natural shoreline sites on the warm, dry side of Maui and planning every inch of 18.5 acres of beachfront land to create a resort complex of exceptional accommodations and services so fanciful and spectacular that everyone who sees it is awed and captivated by both the natural and the manmade beauty.

Christopher B. Hemmeter turned $80 million into the Hyatt Regency Maui resort on magnificent Kaanapali Beach. Part of the reason so much money was spent is that some astounding feats were required. For instance, in creating the grounds and the setting for a half-acre swimming pool and more than a mile of streams, lagoons, seven spectacular waterfalls, grottoes, and a genuine Swan Lake, Hemmeter brought to Maui 22,000 square feet of artificial lava rock made by a firm in Irvine, California, at a cost of $1 million, and combined it with 10,000 tons of the local lava rock. Some would say this is the classic instance of someone bringing coal to Newcastle. Why was this done? Because Hemmeter felt that the local stuff wasn't good enough; the edges were too sharp and the rock too coarse for his future guests to be able to climb and sit on comfortably.

There's more. A collection of art valued at over $2 million is scattered throughout the gardens, along with 38 different varieties of trees, 40 types of shrubs, and 23 different kinds of ground cover plants and vines. The art collection is also scattered through the atrium lobby, which is open to the sky, and in the corridors of the main floor as well.

The view to dine by in the Swan Court is superb. One entire side of this candlelighted restaurant is actually a 30 foot-high opening on the edge of manmade Swan Lake. The lake is fed by three waterfalls, and there is a graceful Japanese bridge at the far end. As you listen to soft piano music and dine on your selections from the Continental menu (which also features some delightful Hawaiian variations), you will most likely experience the ultimate in satisfaction.

Among the specialties are Fresh Island *Eichenholz* (fillet of fish baked on a plate of oak wood) and Veal Cutlet *aux Morilles*. For dessert, look at the cart and decide, or do as we did: order the large, luscious strawberries, glazed and then dipped in rich dark chocolate.

During the day, the Swan Court is open until 11 A.M. for breakfast. And what a breakfast! Even compared with the massive breakfast buffet spreads we saw in Scandinavia, the offerings here surpass anything we've seen both in quantity and richness. Not only are there many varieties of danish and other kinds of breakfast pastries and breads, but there is also a wide assortment of everything else—eggs, sausages, bacon, fruits, yogurt with all the toppings, cereals (including a Swiss cold cereal mixed with fresh fruits), and even miso soup.

We'll let a quote from the menu summarize our feelings for this view to dine by experience: "With regal bearing and white downy plumage, the swan is a creature of legend, a symbol of fragile, ethereal beauty. We think of swans on still lakes beside Rhine castles. . . . With the species Mute Swan and Australian Black Swan, the Hyatt Regency Maui celebrates these wonderous creatures at Swan Court."

ILLINOIS
CHICAGO

Ciel Bleu

Mayfair Regent
181 East Lake Shore Drive
Chicago
Illinois 60611
Telephones: 312–951–2864 or 787–8500

All major credit cards
Breakfast, lunch, and dinner
Reservations requested
Jacket required
Liquor served
Dinner: $40 to $50
    full 3 courses, without wine
Lunch: $17 to $22
Chef: Dominique Fortin
Maitre d': Pierre Robert

Ciel Bleu

This beautiful dining spot is on the 19th floor of the elegant Mayfair Regent Hotel, overlooking Lake Michigan, and only a few steps away from what is called "The Magnificent Mile" along the lake and the elegant Tower Place shopping and residential complex.

The restaurant's dominant feature is the view, which can be enjoyed from just about any seat. Try to sit next to the massive windows lining the eastern and northern walls. Somehow these give you the feeling of floating above the city. To the east, neighboring buildings stand out in sharp relief against the background of Lake Michigan. To the north is an urban landscape: Lake Shore Drive, Chicago's scenic highway, curving gently into the distance with luxury high rises marking the way as far as the eye can see. To the east lies parkland, beach, and shoreline, the huge expanse of the lake giving a sense of infinite distance. Stretching to the north, the clear, crisp lines of the city begin to blur, and the color blends into a soft blue haze.

The view at night—twinkling lights of the skyline, streaks of white and red from the lights of the automobiles on the drive, and street lights illuminating the park and the shoreline—is also very exciting.

Ciel Bleu offers Continental cuisine. It is open for breakfast from 7 A.M. until 10:30 A.M. (when some businesspeople meet to start the day), for lunch from 11:30 A.M. until 2 P.M., and for dinner beginning at 6 P.M., with the last sitting at 9:30 P.M.

The decor of Ciel Bleu, which means blue sky, enhances the view. It has soft rose floral-pattern table linens, fine lead crystal stemware, fine silver and china, and beautiful Palladian style mirrors along the wall reflecting everything inside and out.

Pat Bruno, food critic for the *Chicago Sun-Times*, has said, "the food is more than a match for the view," and awarded it a maximum four stars. Praise has come from other quarters as well—in 1981, the "Outstanding Dinner of the Year" award from *Chaine de Rotisseurs*, and, in 1984, the "Dinner of the Year" title from the International Wine and Food Society of Chicago. Among the esteemed entrées are Veal Medallion with Morel Mushroom Sauce and Albufira Rice, Ragout of Lobster and Sole with Vegetables covered with Tarragon-Lobster Sauce, and Sautéed Fresh Goose Liver with Mache Salad. Among the desserts are White Chocolate Mousse Cake with Raspberry *Coulis* and *Le Feuillette* of Fresh Berries in Caramel Cream Sauce.

The guests are as varied as the cuisine. Of course, the leading businesspeople come here, as do nearby residents of the elegant waterfront buildings. There are also out-of-towners, from all parts of the United States, and many parts of the world.

The Pinnacle

Holiday Inn Lake Shore
644 Lake Shore Drive
Chicago
Illinois 60611
Telephone: 312–943–0653

All major credit cards
Dinner
Reservations necessary
Jacket required
Liquor served
Dinner: $15 to $25
full 3 courses, without wine
Chef: Glen Brittingham
Maitre d': Pedro Rodriguez

The Pinnacle atop the Holiday Inn Lake Shore on Chicago's famous Gold Coast is the city's only revolving rooftop restaurant.

While dining in the glass-enclosed restaurant at softly-lighted tables enhanced by richly appointed burgundy velvet decor and crystal chandeliers, it is possible to enjoy a gourmet meal and vintage wines while at the same time experiencing a breathtaking view of the Chicago skyline. The picture-postcard scene encompasses the twinkling lights and architectural brilliance of the Loop's corporate skyscrapers, thirty-five miles of Chicago's lakeside beach bordered by the elegant apartment buildings that dominate Chicago's legendary Lake Shore Drive, colorful yachts and sailboats anchored in Burnham and Delmont Harbors, and notable Chicago landmarks such as Grant Park and its majestic Buckingham Fountain, the Navy Pier, McCormick Place, and more.

This plushly carpeted dining room seats up to 180 people and makes a full rotation each hour. All diners, no matter where they are seated, have a panoramic view through the floor-to-ceiling windows that wrap this spacious room. There are even tables set on the perimeter of the revolving area, at windowside, for those who do not want to be on a moving platform. Piano music helps create a pleasant atmosphere during dinner. Among the main dishes served here are Shrimp *De Jonghe,* Steak Diane, *Filet Mignon Cordon Rouge,* Rack of Lamb (for two), and an assortment of fresh fish that changes daily.

The Pinnacle

LOUISIANA
NEW ORLEANS

Commander's Palace

1403 Washington Avenue
   at Coliseum Street
New Orleans
Louisiana 70130
Telephone: 504–899–8221

All major credit cards
Lunch and dinner every day,
   breakfast Saturday and Sunday
Reservations recommended
Jacket required
Liquor served
Dinner: $23 to $29
   full 3 courses, without wine
Lunch: $10 to $17
Chef: Emeril Lagasse
Maitre d': George Rico

What constitutes the best view here is in dispute. Some feel that this fine old 1880 restaurant and its building in the heart of the New Orleans Garden District is the primary thing of beauty. Others feel that the view of the interior dining court, by candlelight at night, is the more enchanting. We like both.

The structure of Commander's Palace is Victorian, with a turret, columns, and lots of gingerbread, painted bright turquoise with a crisp white trim. In 1880, Emile Commander established the only restaurant patronized by the distinguished families of the Garden District, the famed part of the city where George W. Cable entertained Mark Twain and where Jefferson Davis spent his last days. Mr. Commander chose the corner of Washington Avenue and Coliseum Street, a site that had once been a part of the J.F.E. Livaudais Plantation and later was the *faubourg* of Lafayette (which was subsequently engulfed by the westward expansion of the city of New Orleans in 1854). By 1900, Commander's Palace, fully a part of a bustling metropolis, was attracting gourmets from around the world.

It was during the twenties, under different management, that Commander's developed what might be called a spicier reputation. River-boat captains frequented the place, and sporting gentlemen brought their beautiful "ladies" for a rendezvous in the private dining rooms upstairs. Downstairs, however, the main dining room, with its separate entrance, was maintained as a place of impeccable respectability for family meals after church and for other special occasions.

The present owners, Ella, Dottie, Dick, and John Brennan, took over in 1974 and gave the splendid old landmark a new look. They decided to design rooms and settings indoors which complemented and enhanced the lovely outdoor setting—the deep green garden in back and the lovely patio with its fountain—creating an ambience that played up the sunlight and the garden atmosphere of the restaurant's setting. Walls were torn out and replaced with walls of glass, inviting the views to become part of the decor. Paintings were commissioned for each room to specially suit each one's particular color and design.

Commander's cuisine combines the best of the New Orleans Creole heritage with the creative concepts of modern cooking. Everything is as fresh as it can possibly be: seafood, meats, fruits, and vegetables. Among our favorites from a large and elaborate menu are, to start, Oyster Dome Soup, then Veal Chop Tchoupitoulas or Soft Shell Crabs Charone, and, for dessert, a Bread Pudding Soufflé.

Every Saturday and Sunday there's Commander's Jazz Brunch, with muted jazz played throughout the restaurant by Alvin Alcorn, an old-time jazz great, and his groups. It's a festive atmosphere, with balloons everywhere and a special Jazz Brunch menu. Generous portions of everything are featured.

Le Jardin

The Westin Canal Place
100 Rue Iberville
New Orleans
Louisiana 70130
Telephone: 504–566–7006

All major credit cards
Dinner
Reservations necessary
Jacket required
Liquor served
Dinner: $25 to $35
*   full 3 courses, without wine*
Chef: Edward Fitzpatrick
Maitre d': Manual Estrada

Here, in what had opened in 1984 as the Hotel Iberville but is now known as the Westin Canal Place, is a restaurant with one of the best views of New Orleans, situated on the 11th floor of the building which towers above New Orleans's shopping complex, Canal Place.

Called Le Jardin, this restaurant is an elegant room blending the styles of Victorian England and Frank Lloyd Wright, with spans of golden wood, sparkling marble, china-filled hutches, brocade-backed chairs, and palm-filled Chinese urns. Le Jardin is more like a European dining salon than a garden.

The most exciting part of the decor is the splendid view of the Mississippi River through the vast spread of glass that surrounds the dining room on two sides; the glass wall continues, unobstructed, through the full length of the lobby of the hotel. Adding to the dinner charm is soft piano music, the fashionably dressed guests, and the tuxedoed waiters.

Le Jardin's cuisine is a blend of modern and traditional French. Among the delightful entrées are Lobster Thermidor, Fillet of Dover Sole marinated in raspberry vinegar and hazelnut oil on a *coulis* of fresh papaya, and Fillet of Beef baked in pastry with Bearnaise and Bordelaise sauces lightly applied.

The desserts are grand! The three favorites, in order of popularity (according to Chef Fitzpatrick), are Pecan Cheesecake, Praline Soufflé, and *Creme Brulée au Chocolat.*

Afternoon tea, or a bit of caviar and champagne, are available at Chic Celebration, the lobby lounge. A violin and harp are played at tea time, and music from a grand piano can be heard in the evening.

The Rainforest

Rooftop of
The New Orleans Hilton
Poydras at the Mississippi River
New Orleans
Louisiana 70140
Telephone: 504–561–0500
　　　　　Ext. RAIN (7246)

All major credit cards
Lunch
Reservations not required
Jacket not required
Liquor served
Lunch: $5 to $8
Chef: Kathy Vogel
Maitre d': Dawn Marino

　　　　We find this view down the Mississippi River one of our favorites, taking in the crescent-shaped bend in the river and the old French Quarter of the city. Sometimes you find yourself so enchanted by the view you forget to eat.

　　　　The Rainforest used to be a place for evening dancing, but now it is also open for lunch, and the management has done something very interesting with that. Featured is something called the Prudent Diet, "a creation of the Hilton Chef under the guidelines of the American Heart Association. The Prudent Diet is a well-balanced buffet comprised of low-fat, reduced-sodium, low-cholesterol, low-calorie, and high-fiber selections." Among the items to be discovered are Indonesian Gado Gado, Ricotta Lasagna, Romaine and Radish Salad, Yogurt Mint Soup, Tabouli, Broiled Tofu with Mirin Sauce, and Tofutti.

　　　　This restaurant, located on the 29th floor, is a welcome respite from the excitement of New Orleans. But not for long—as darkness falls, it too becomes part of the city pulse, with cocktails, dancing, and the lights of the city and the river becoming positively electric.

MAINE

KENNEBUNKPORT

Olde Grist Mill

1 Mill Lane
Kennebunkport
Maine 04046
Telephone: 207–967–4781/5670

All major credit cards
Dinner
Reservations necessary
Jacket not required
Liquor served
Dinner: $11 to $25
　　　full 3 courses, without wine
Chef: Marco P. Ramirez
Owner and Maitre d':
　　　David F. Lombard

Although it hardly looks like a fortress, the Olde Grist Mill was used by natives of the "Port" as a temporary redoubt against hostile Indians some 200 years ago. Except for the addition of some replacement shingles, a cupola, and minor repairs, the Mill is the same as it was then.

The present owner, Dave Lombard, told us that his mother bought the mill from her father in 1940. Dave has been running the restaurant since 1965, so this is, to quote him, "probably the longest-running business in southern Maine that is owned and operated by the same family."

The building was placed on the Register of Historic Buildings in 1973 and is the *only* tide-water (operated on the change of height of the tidal waters) grist mill in the nation. Old mills and millstones are becoming a rarity. The Olde Grist Mill is on a little estuary about a half-mile above the Kennebunk River; it is picturesquely weatherbeaten and situated on the edge of a small stream where the inflowing waters of the river are imprisoned by a dam. This mill had ground corn unceasingly for more than two centuries and had been in full operation until recent years.

The interior has changed little, too. It has the old scales, the hopper, and the slender little elevator which carried the grist up in an endless chain of little carriers. On the wall is a lovely old map of the northeastern coast of North America as it was in 1821, with corrections and changes noted by the millers through the years. The floor of wide boards is brown and polished; the hand-hewn beams and crosspieces supported by ship's knees are browned with age; and the wooden blinds, true to the 1740's, swing upon the inside of the window instead of in the open.

The Olde Grist Mill is called "Maine's Most Unique Eating Place" because of its Colonial atmosphere and its delicious Johnny Cake, Baked Indian Pudding, and other old fashioned dishes in New England tradition.

David tells us that the favorites from a bountiful menu are Poached Salmon Doria, Baked Stuffed Shrimp Macadamia, and Steak *au Poivre*. The dessert menu is overwhelming; among the favorites are Baked Indian Pudding (the house specialty), Deep Dish Apple Pie à la Mode, and a selection of about a dozen different ice cream desserts, including all kinds of sundaes and parfaits.

MASSACHUSETTS
BOSTON

The Dining Room of The Ritz-Carlton

15 Arlington Street
Boston
Massachusetts 02117
Telephone: 617–536–5700

All major credit cards
Breakfast, lunch, dinner, and Sunday brunch
Reservations advised
Jacket required
Dinner: $22 to $30
  full 3 courses, without wine
Lunch: $16 to $20
Chef: John Vyhnanek
Maitre d': Joseph Lucherini

The Ritz-Carlton in Boston is one of a group of Ritz-Carlton hotels in the United States that prides itself on being deserved of the Ritz name. Colgate Holmes, president of the Ritz-Carlton Hotels of North America, believes sincerely that his hotels must earn their reputations each day. The lovely dining room of the Ritz-Carlton, Boston, can help boost the hotel's good name. The personal dining room of King Ludwig of Bavaria was used as a model for this room. The cobalt blue which beautifully enriches the restaurant's decor has come to be known as "Ritz-Carlton blue." The signature cobalt glasses were inspired by the cobalt blue in the original chandeliers installed when the hotel was built in 1927; these chandeliers still hang there today.

This is a sophisticated dining room in a hotel that has firmly stood by its dress code throughout the years. Some say it is more Bostonian than Boston itself. This has meant turning away movie stars and other celebrities who arrive in jeans or outlandish apparel. We're very prejudiced and think it's great that the elegance and tranquility that is so respected here is not allowed to be destroyed.

From the expansive windows in the Dining Room is a view that only the Ritz-Carlton can offer—a panorama of the Public Garden's flowers in the spring and ice skaters on the pond in winter. The Public Garden's fleet of swan boats, each one of which looks like a raft with a giant swan in back, is also visible, weather permitting.

The dining room offers superb Continental cuisine. On the menu cover is a reproduction of a beautiful painting of the Ritz-Carlton, the Garden, and its pond, by Kamil Kubik. Inside, the dinner menu features a wide range of fine items. We are told that the favorite main courses here are Lobster with Whiskey and Sautéed Dover Sole. Starred items on the menu are the chef's selections of light and nutritious dishes; some of them are, as appetizers, *Saumon Marine Norvegien, Sauce Moutarde* (marinated fresh salmon with mustard dill sauce), and Oysters or Little Neck clams in Season, and, for soup, Gazpacho *Andalous.* For your main course, Medallions of Venison with cracked peppercorns and currants, Broiled Boston Scrod, and Grilled Thin Veal Cutlet with chive butter are all starred.

A grand brunch, on Sundays from 11 A.M. until 1:30 P.M., is accompanied by chamber music from the Nuages Chamber Players. The pianist at dinner and at lunch plays a combination of popular melodies and classics from the stage and screen. At lunch, on Saturday, there is a fashion show—another attractive view to dine by.

CAMBRIDGE

The Empress

Hyatt Regency Cambridge
Overlooking Boston
575 Memorial Drive
Cambridge
Massachusetts 02139
Telephone: 617–492–1234

All major credit cards
Dinner and Sunday brunch
Reservations requested
Jacket required
Liquor served
Dinner: $18 to $25
Chef: Steve Jayson
Maitre d': Y.P. Lou

Conscious that Boston is a pretty city to look at, this restaurant takes advantage of it from the ground up. A glass elevator takes guests to the 14th floor and a grand restaurant, the Empress. At the top, there is a spectacular view of the city's skyline.

The Empress has exquisite Oriental decor and serves gourmet Oriental specialties from a long and varied list. According to a local critic, the Empress is the "most ambient" restaurant in the Boston area.

Most popular is the Sunday brunch, which features Oriental, Continental, and a bit of New American cuisine. Also on Sundays guests are invited to see another, most unusual, view . . . they are encouraged to enter the kitchen, which is actually an authentic recreation of a Chinese kitchen, where they can watch the chefs prepare the lavish specialties offered that day.

Dinner is served nightly, Monday through Thursday and Sunday from 6 P.M. until 10:30 P.M.; on Friday and Saturday dinner is from 6 P.M. until 11 P.M.; Sunday Brunch is served from 11 A.M. until 3 P.M.

DEERFIELD

The Main Dining Room of
The Deerfield Inn

The Street
Deerfield
Massachusetts 01342
Telephone: 413–774–5587

All major credit cards
Breakfast, lunch, and dinner
Reservations required
Jacket required
Liquor served
Dinner: $20 to $27
*   full 3 courses, without wine*
Lunch: $9 to $12
Chef: Chris Opalenik
Maitre d': Georgiann Kopf

Dining at The Deerfield Inn gives one a glimpse of life as it was in Colonial America. Located in the center of historic Deerfield, a town with 12 beautifully restored museum houses, the inn is so well preserved that it looks much as it did when it was opened in 1884. The village of Old Deerfield has been designated a National Historic Site by the federal government, making it an authentic living monument to early New England life. This is only fitting, considering that the village was settled about 300 years ago and was once an outpost in the wilderness of Colonial America.

The inn has been modernized, with air-conditioning, 23 deluxe guest rooms, a cocktail lounge, two bars, a coffee shop, and a dining room. The decor features glistening mahogany and cherrywood tables, Queen Anne, Chippendale, and Federal-style chairs, oriental rugs, floral draperies, and brass chandeliers.

The luncheon menu includes traditional favorites such as Broiled Fresh Haddock, Scallops, Shish-Kebab, and daily specials featuring a *Crêpe du Jour* and fresh fish from New England waters. Dinner features more specialized gourmet dishes such as New England Baked Shrimp, Veal Orloff, *Tournedos au Poivre,* and Boneless Breast of Chicken Kiev. Among the desserts are Indian Pudding, Brandied Custard Bread Pudding, and a Queen Anne Torte.

MICHIGAN
DEARBORN

The Early American Room

The Dearborn Inn
20301 Oakwood Boulevard
Dearborn
Michigan 48124
Telephone: 313–271–2700

All major credit cards
Lunch: Monday through Friday;
*   dinner: Monday through Saturday*
Reservations preferred
Jacket preferred
Liquor served
Dinner: $15 to $30
*   full 3 courses, without wine*
Chef: Kevin Corcoran

Henry Ford (1863-1947) loved automobiles and the transportation industry. He also loved Georgian architecture. When he built the Dearborn Inn in 1931 he combined the two. Located across from what was then the Ford Airport, it is said to be the world's first airport hotel.

Mr. Ford took an active part in the design of the Inn, personally overseeing the development of many of its unique, charming features—such as the Alexandria Ballroom on the second floor. It's reported that Mr. Ford and his wife Clara led 250 guests around the ballroom in a grand march which ended with one of Mr. Ford's favorite pastimes: an evening of American dancing, followed by a buffet supper.

Because Mr. Ford admired the hospitality of New England and southern inns he made certain that the Dearborn Inn offered that same old-fashioned, warm, personal service. Making the guests feel at home has sustained the Inn for over 50 years.

The Inn and the adjacent Colonial homes, which can be seen from the Early American Room, reflect Henry Ford's fondness for (and, indeed, his involvement in) American history.

The Early American Dining Room, with its rose-print wallpaper and draperies, and its chandeliers, has an air of elegance and grace. Luncheon and dinner entrées served here include early American dishes, many of which come from Michigan and the Great Lakes region. A guest may start the meal with an appetizer such as Michigan Bean Soup. Main dishes include Roast Prime Rib of Western Beef and a large array of tasty seafood: Fillet of Fresh Scrod, Whitefish from the Great Lakes, Fresh Gulf Shrimp, Trout from Lake Superior, Golden Pickerel, and Great Lakes Perch. Popular at lunch are the wide selections of sandwiches including Prime Rib, Club, and Reuben.

A special children's menu with smaller and, for them, entertaining items, includes "Fife and Drum" drum sticks and the "Minute Man" hamburger, both served with French fries and milk.

On Friday night a Seafood Fantasy is served until 10 P.M. And on Saturday, traditional American cuisine is featured until 11 P.M.

DETROIT

The Summit
Hotel Westin
Renaissance Center
Detroit
Michigan 48243
Telephone: 313–567–2300

All major credit cards
Lunch, dinner,
*   and Sunday brunch*
Reservations required
Jacket not required
Liquor served
Dinner: $14.95 to $21.95
*   full 3 courses, without wine*
Lunch: $5.95 to $12.95
Chef: Beat Richei
Maitre d': Tom Dupar

The Summit is a trilevel restaurant and lounge located atop the Westin Hotel in the Renaissance Center of Detroit. Its position on the 71st through 73d floors of the tower provides a spectacular view; two of its levels revolve almost imperceptibly. Diners can see the buildings of downtown Detroit directly below, as well as the Detroit River, with its constant flow of varied shipping traffic, and, to the south across the river, the town of Windsor in the Ontario province of Canada.

The Summit is a fantastic spot to enjoy beautiful sunsets. And, as evening falls, the mood changes and the city lights become a lovely accompaniment to a fine meal. Especially pretty is the strand of lights which adorn the Ambassador Bridge to Canada.

The Summit menu includes a wide variety of fresh seafood, poultry, and meat dishes from different regions of North America. The Westin Hotels, in its system-wide competition, awarded the Summit the Silver Spoon Award for fine dining at lunch and brunch.

Among the specialties on the menu is the Great Combo, which features Lobster Tail and *Petit Mignon.* For dessert there is the Summit Orbiter, Harvey Wallbanger Ice Cream sprinkled with Chocolate Chips, topped with whipped cream, and served in a container with dry ice beneath it for a spectacular presentation. The favorite drink is the Summit Spinner—blended rum, two brandies, Triple Sec, and fruit juices, served in a souvenir glass which is a replica of the Westin, the world's tallest hotel.

The Westin Hotel is 710 feet above Jefferson Avenue. To reach the restaurant at the top, take the Sky Lobby elevator which takes off from the third floor of the hotel, the Ontario level. Since the hotel is very popular for conventions, make your reservation well in advance if you want to be sure to get one of the limited number of seats available in the Summit.

GRAND RAPIDS

Cygnus Restaurant

Grand Plaza Hotel
Pearl at Monroe
Grand Rapids
Michigan 49503
Telephone: 616–776–6145

All major credit cards
Dinner
Reservations necessary
Jacket required
Liquor served
Dinner: $30 to $50
 full 3 courses, without wine
Chef: Rudolf Van Nunen
Maitre d': Erich Ploetz

The Cygnus Restaurant opened in 1983 on the 28th floor of the 29-story glass-enclosed tower of the Grand Plaza Hotel, the tallest building between Chicago and Detroit.

Cygnus is named for the swan constellation seen through the glass roof of the restaurant. Diners have a spectacular view of the city of Grand Rapids, including the Grand River and the Gerald R. Ford Presidential Museum. To the far west, the outline of sand dunes along Lake Michigan is discernable.

When readers of *West Michigan Magazine 1985* were asked, "If you could have only one more meal in West Michigan, where would you go?", the overwhelming response was Cygnus. It was also selected by the readers as the best restaurant in Grand Rapids and as the restaurant having the best service and atmosphere.

No wonder. Cygnus is upscale and elegant, a place where caviar is served with double cream and veal with sweetbreads. It is also expensive; $100 per couple is not unusual. Luckily, you get what you pay for. The room is dramatic. The walls and most of the ceiling are made of glass. A pink marble dance floor is surrounded by tall and feathery papier-mâché palm trees. The tables are set with maroon and white linens, the napkins folded like swans. The wine glasses are sparkling Romanian crystal.

Chef Van Nunen takes pride in his achievements and works extensively with local farmers to get them to deliver the freshest products available. Fish is procured fresh from Michigan streams.

Cygnus is famous for its Gin Tomato Soup à la Ritz, prepared for two at your table ($9). This unique concoction is said to have originated at the Ritz in Berlin. The entrées are imaginative, too, ranging in price from $18 to $24. Among them are Partridge with Truffle, Cooked Apple filled with chestnut purée, topped with two cooked chestnuts, wild rice, and asparagus spears, Noisettes of Veal with Sweetbreads, a dish featuring woven strips of salmon and whitefish in a sauce made of pink champagne, butter, and soup stock, and Veal Medallions and Fresh Shrimp in Green Chervil Sauce.

The desserts are artistic as well. A plate of chocolate mousse flowers and a delicate chocolate butterfly is decorated with a pale and delicious green mint sauce. Butter Pecan Ice Cream is served on a thin pastry island floating in a sea of fresh raspberry sauce.

ST. CLAIR

St. Clair Inn
500 North Riverside
St. Clair
Michigan 48079
Telephone: 313-329-2222

All major credit cards
Breakfast, lunch, and dinner
Reservations recommended
Jacket not required
Liquor served
Dinner: $10 to $21
  full 3 courses, without wine
Lunch: $5 to $9.50
Chef: Warren Zimmer
Proprietor: Donald W. Reynolds

Diners at the St. Clair Inn are treated to a constant panorama of lake and ocean steamers on the St. Clair River, which connects Lake Huron with Lake St. Clair. The quiet majesty of these giant boats, which come from many lands, as they pass closely by the dining room windows, never fails to awe the guests at dinner. The American shipping channel for the Great Lakes is only 30 feet off the dock. Guests claim that the view from here is the best in the state of Michigan.

This is a cozy country inn whose manager, Michael J. Laporte, is proud of the food served here. Among the favorite main dishes are Walleye Pike and Bay Scallops. For dessert, try the strawberry pie.

MINNESOTA
MINNEAPOLIS

The Orion Room

5000 IDS Tower
Minneapolis
Minnesota 55402
Telephone: 612–349–6250

All major credit cards
Lunch and Sunday brunch
Reservations preferred
Jacket required
Liquor served
Dinner: $8.95 to $22.50
full 3 courses,
without wine
Brunch: $15.95
Chef: Charles A. Venables
General Manager:
Martin J. O'Dowd

Recipient of the *Twin Cities Reader* Best View Award, the Orion Room is located on the west side of the 50th floor of the IDS Center. It offers an excellent view of Minneapolis and its suburbs during the day and an unsurpassed view of the city at sunset. By night, twinkling lights far below extend to the horizon in all directions.

The room itself is a beautiful place to dine. It is contemporary and sophisticated, with a decor influenced by classical motifs. The unique angles of the faceted IDS Building are used as a recurring theme throughout the restaurant. The decor features gray and teal with a terra-cotta accent. A tiered seating arrangement uses mahogany chairs upholstered in pinstriped gray wool and teal banquettes to seat 165 diners. The panoramic view is available to diners through floor-to-ceiling windows and is reflected by etched mirrors so that all may see it.

The Orion Room features the best in the new trends of cooking while retaining many old favorites, including Roast Prime Ribs of Beef, a lobster and fillet combination, and its famous Wild Rice Soup. The new menu features regional American cuisine and a variety of fresh cookery that reveals a wealth of tradition and history behind each dish. Appetizers include Sliced Salmon with Mustard and Dill Sauce, and entrées include Roast Duckling with Orange and Blueberry Sauce, Roast Rack of Lamb, and Fresh Broiled Walleye Pike. The American Field Salad is a nice accompaniment to almost anything you order. Among the desserts are seasonal fresh fruit tarts and *Gateau Marjolaine*.

If you're in Minneapolis on a Sunday, the place for Sunday brunch with a view is certainly the Orion Room. The spread of things to eat is endless and very good, not only with standard brunch items such as eggs, breads, and salads, but also with a lot of special things that wealthy gourmand brunch-goers would enjoy, ranging from champagne, Mimosas, and Bloody Marys to smoked salmon, pâtés, sliced turkey breast, an assortment of cheeses, and all kinds of fresh fruits. The dessert spread is amazing—French pastries, cheesecake, and apple flambé! If you are too filled for a dessert or two, settle for a plump strawberry dipped in white chocolate!

MISSOURI
KANSAS CITY

The American Restaurant

Atop Hall's Crown Center
2450 Grand Avenue
Kansas City
Missouri 64108
Telephone: 816–471–8050

All major credit cards
Dinner
Reservations suggested
Jacket required
Liquor served
Dinner: $9.75 to $17.95
  full 3 courses, without wine
Chef: Kenn Dunn
General Manager: Rolf Wetzel

Just minutes away from the heart of downtown Kansas City is Crown Center, a complex built largely through the inspiration of the late Joyce Hall, founder and president of Hallmark Cards. We are prejudicially fond of this place, because we had the unique pleasure of working with Mr. Hall on its design. Far more than just another shopping center, this complex sought to display a panorama of American enterprise through its shops and restaurants as well as through all of its public spaces and halls. It seems to have succeeded; after it was built, Crown Center became the model for many fine shopping complexes around the world.

The American Restaurant plays an integral part in following through with Hall's concept. It is an excellent reflection of America's finest cookery, offering impeccable service in elegant surroundings. The view looks over downtown Kansas City and the 10-acre Crown Center Square from approximately five stories up. During the warm summer months, the grass terraces, fountains, and flowers on the Square provide extra color. During the holiday season, the Square has a 70-foot Mayor's Christmas Tree which, when seen with the 20,000 twinkling lights on the trees surrounding it, provides a breathtaking spectacle.

The American is an award-winning restaurant, counting among its honors a *Mobil Four Star* rating, the Cartier Award, *Travel/Holiday* Fine Dining Award, the *Wine Spectator* Award of Excellence, and others.

Among the menu highlights are Barbecued Shrimp over Kansas Wheat (as featured by the American Restaurant at the 1984 presidential inaugural celebration) and Lobster in White Wine with Blue Corn Tortillas—a great salute to our American colors! The menu also features such American fare as fresh rainbow trout, creamy brie from Illinois, Kentucky ham, and of course, the celebrated Kansas City Strip.

The American's buffet is set on an immense brass, wood, and beveled glass fixture, laden daily with over 50 diverse and sumptuous offerings including vegetables tossed with farmer's cheese, Duck Salad with Orange Vinaigrette, Red Potato Salad in Hot Mustard Dressing, California Artichokes, Apple and Ham Pâté, Shellfish Salad in Garlic, Basil, and Pine Nuts, and on and on!

The dessert is the grand finale. Included are Chocolate Whiskey Cake, Sugarbush Mountain Maple Mousse, Frozen Hazelnut Soufflé, Candied Ginger Crepes, and the pastry chef's own homemade ice cream.

The American Restaurant is open for dinner from 6 P.M. to 10 P.M. Monday through Thursday, and until 11 P.M. on Friday and Saturday. It's very popular with the citizens of Kansas City and visitors from around the world.

The Crystal Pavilion

Crown Center
25th and Grand Avenue
Kansas City
Missouri 64108
Telephone: 816–471–2003

All major credit cards
Lunch and dinner
Reservations suggested
Dress: casual
Liquor served
Dinner: $18
  full 3 courses, without wine
Lunch: $8
Chef: Keith Fuemmeler
General Manager: Mark Wadsworth

The Crystal Pavilion is a glass-enclosed restaurant stretching out from the Crown Center shops, offering an appealing view of the Crown Center Square through picturesque arched windows in bright and casual surroundings.

Less costly than its neighbor, the American Restaurant, and with a different menu, the Crystal Pavilion has popular appeal for those working and shopping in the Crown Center. During the summer months, the guests enjoy a view of the 10-acre Square and can actually sit in the Square at tables under sun umbrellas, as the restaurant has outdoor seating. At holiday time, the scene is of the big Christmas tree and the colorful lights which reflect so excitingly through the restaurant's crystal canopy.

The menu's highlights include everything from steaks, broiled salmon, and Raspberry Duck to some of the city's best bar appetizers. Lunch is served Monday through Saturday from 11:30 A.M. until 2:30 P.M. Dinner is from 6 P.M. to 10 P.M., Monday through Thursday, and until 11 P.M., Friday and Saturday. The popular Happy Hour is from 4 P.M. to 6 P.M., Monday through Thursday, and until 7 P.M. on Friday.

Skies

Hyatt Regency Kansas City
at Crown Center
2345 McGee Street
Kansas City
Missouri 64108
Telephone: 816–421–1234

All major credit cards
Dinner
Reservations not necessary
Dress: semiformal
Liquor served
Dinner: $13.95 to $24.50
full 3 courses, without wine
Chef: Phil Guttendorf
Manager: Terri Stielow

It is said that on a clear day diners in the Skies revolving restaurant, on the 45th story of the Hyatt Regency Kansas City Hotel, can see as far as twenty miles away. But in case it is cloudy and the exterior view is not at its best, this dining room has a unique substitute—a view of the state's prairie past. Wrapped around the center core of this restaurant-in-the-round is a 360-degree photomural capturing the essence of the Kansas prairie.

In these days when the concept of a revolving restaurant is grand but not unusual, what better improvement could there be but a revolving interior mural? This 186-foot panorama is a horizon-to-horizon vista of the Konza Prairie, the largest untouched area of native prairie tallgrass in the nation, located 100 miles west of Kansas City. So when diners tire of straining to see the new Kansas City airport 20 miles away, they can relax and look back over their shoulders to see "how it used to be."

Dinner at the Skies is a delight. The cuisine features such main dishes as Certified Black Angus Beef, T-Bone, Strip, and Fillet steaks, Blackened Redfish, and *Pollo* Pesto Florentine. A favorite dessert here is Sky High Ice Cream Pie.

NEVADA
INCLINE VILLAGE

Hugo's Rotisserie

Hyatt Lake Tahoe
Country Club Drive and Lakeshore Boulevard
Incline Village
Nevada 89450
Telephone: 702–831–1111

All major credit cards
Dinner
Reservations suggested
Dress: casual
Dinner: $12 to $20
Chef: Yasu Suzuki
Director: Robert Simeone

As Mark Twain wrote upon looking at Lake Tahoe: " . . . The view was always fascinating, bewitching, entrancing. The eye was never tired of gazing, night or day, in calm or storm; it suffered but one grief, and that was that it could not look always, but must close sometime in sleep."

Hugo's picturesque waterfront location, across the street from the Hyatt Lake Tahoe, offers diners an unobstructed view of Lake Tahoe and the surrounding Sierra Mountain Range. The mountains reach to the clouds and remain capped with snow year-round. The lake, which is 1,645 feet deep, 22 miles long, and almost 13 miles wide, can be glassy and clear like a pond or rough with waves crashing on the beach like the ocean.

In *The Saga of Lake Tahoe* writer Edward B. Scott also weighed in with his thoughts on this famous lake: "Brilliant blues, vivid greens, intense ultra marines, magnificent deep indigo with delicate shadings of purple, violet, and cobalt. These and other combinations of chromatic colors and tints may be seen in the crystal purity of Tahoe's snow waters."

The cuisine is a delight, too, having been awarded three stars in the *Mobil* guide. The house specialty is the spit-roasted fresh duckling.

NEW HAMPSHIRE
NORTH WOODSTOCK

Clement Room of
The Woodstock Inn

Route 3, Main Street
P.O. Box 118
North Woodstock
New Hampshire 03262
Telephone: 603–745–3951

All major credit cards
Breakfast, lunch, and dinner
Reservations necessary on
  Friday and Saturday
Jacket not required
Liquor served
Dinner: $9.50 to $18.50
  full 3 courses, without wine
Lunch: the same
Chefs: Scott Rice and Erik Nelson
Maitre d': Eileen Rice

The Clement Room at the Woodstock Inn is a glass-enclosed petticoat porch open year-round for breakfast, lunch, and dinner. It is named for the gentleman who lived in the home for sixty years and who was the town's postmaster.

The Inn contains an interesting hodgepodge of New Hampshire history. For example, just recently Scott and Eileen Rice, the owners, bought Lincoln's original railroad station and moved it from its previous location and attached it to the Inn. Then they added a few other pieces and parts, such as the 100-year-old four-station barber shop behind the bar, old sewing machines (now used as tables), and seats from the old Lakeport Opera House. All this plus a new outdoor patio for dining on warm summer days contributes to a most unusual view to dine by.

Called the "Woodstock Station," the menu here is an entertaining bill of fare. The categories in it are in keeping with the railroad theme: "All Aboard for Appetizers" features Arti Choo Choo, artichokes marinated in pesto and baked with melted cheese. Other appetizers include Railroad Ties, which are fried cheese sticks with a Dijon mustard sauce; Box Car of Shrimp—"peelum and eatum," with cocktail sauce; Split Rails, a half pound of spicy barbecued pork ribs; and Frog that got Caught on the Tracks, frog legs sautéed in butter and garlic.

Under "Station Soups," there are the Hobo Soup of the Day, the Montrealer (baked French onion soup), and Maine Central (seafood chowder "that's loaded!").

The Station Salads include the Acapulco Express, a salad in a flour tortilla with chili and avocado slices; and the Train Just Pasta, orzo pasta salad with shrimps and artichokes.

"Sandwiched Between the Tracks" includes the Crabby Conductor, the Fall River Connection, the Smoke-Stacked Sandwich, the Cattle Crossing, and the Rushin' Reuben.

"The Main Line" items include Coastal Express, with scallops, shrimp, and fish fried in a Newburg sauce with a crumb crust, Twenty Tiny Twisted Tunnels, which is mushrooms and Gruyere tortellinis topped with pesto and marinara, and a Station Steak, charbroiled and lots more.

In the dessert area, the names are truly crazy. Waffles offered include Before the Tornado, Somewhere Over the Rainbow, There's No Place Like Home, If I Only Had a Brain, and the Wicked Witch's Waffle.

This, as you gather, makes your meal enjoyable, but we must point out that the food is seriously good. Among the favorites are Roast Duckling, Clement's Classic (beef tenderloin layered with crabmeat and asparagus with Hollandaise Sauce), and the hand-cut veal, the most popular of which is Veal Oscar, which is crabmeat, asparagus, and Bearnaise Sauce.

NEW JERSEY
HIGHLANDS

Bahrs Landing

Two Bay Avenue
Highlands
New Jersey 07732
Telephone: 201–872–1245

All major credit cards
Lunch and dinner
Reservations not required
Jacket not required
Liquor served
Dinner: Moderate
Chef: Gordon Dingman
Proprietor: Ray Cosgrove

It is said that this is the approximate spot where the first white man—Henry Hudson—set foot on the soil of New Jersey. He landed his ship, the *Half Moon,* here on September 5, 1609, as part his historic journey in the New World.

The Landing has been a comfortable, down-to-earth restaurant ever since it was started by the Bahrs in 1918. It features a sweeping view. Behind it are the Highlands of Navesink, "world-famous portals at the gateway to the United States." Atop these hills, which are the highest elevation on the East Coast, are the famous Twin Lights lighthouses, the last lingering bit of America visible as ships sail east, and the first to be sighted by ships arriving from Europe. To the north is desolate Sandy Hook, separating the waters of the Atlantic Ocean from the broad stretches of Lower New York Bay. Beyond that is the sketchy outline of Coney Island. At night it appears to be a distant fairyland floating in the sky. As you dine you may see great passenger liners, warships, barges, sailing ships, and many other kinds of vessels moving in and out of view. Directly in front of the restaurant is the Shrewsbury River, noted for fishing and crabbing.

There is more history attached to this spot. It was here that what was called the American Riviera began—in the late 17th century the wealthy patrons of New Amsterdam had their summer cottages on the slopes of the Highlands of Navesink. Many of the scenes in James Fenimore Cooper's *The Pilot* took place here. And Gertrude Ederle, the first woman to swim the English Channel, was taught to swim at a point less than a hundred feet from the restaurant.

The building that contains the restaurant was originally a boat house built in 1890. It was eventually beached, put on pilings, and a second floor was added. From 1903, it was a hangout for fishermen.

A typical seafood restaurant, the menu features clam chowder, lobsters, coleslaw, and hot biscuits. For dessert, a picturesque Mile High Pie (lemon chiffon) is a good choice.

PRINCETON

Greenhouse Restaurant
Nassau Inn

Palmer Square
Princeton
New Jersey 08542
Telephone: 609–921–7500

All major credit cards
Breakfast, lunch, and dinner
Reservations suggested
Jacket not required
Liquor served
Dinner: $5 to $15
　full 3 courses, without wine
Lunch: $5 to $10
Chef: Tony Sindaco
Food and Beverage Director: Kevin M. Howard

The broad windows of the Nassau Inn's airy Greenhouse Restaurant overlook picturesque Palmer Square in the college town of Princeton. The square's diversity of Colonial architecture tells the story, in part, of Princeton's place in American history.

The Nassau Inn, which is now an Omni Hotel, was built in 1937 by Edgar Palmer, who had a vision of a town square containing apartment, office, and retail buildings, with the Nassau Inn as its hub and the beautiful Gothic spires of Princeton University as the backdrop.

The cuisine is excellent and reasonably priced. It won two silver medals at the 1984 Culinary Olympics in Frankfurt, West Germany. Among the favorite main dishes are Steamed Turbot with Basil Cream Sauce and fresh Tomatoes and Sautéed Veal Medallions with Sun-Dried Tomatoes, fresh Basil, and Dijon Cream Sauce.

SEA BRIGHT

The RiverHouse on the Quay

280 Ocean Avenue
Sea Bright
New Jersey 07760
Telephone: 201–842–1994

All major credit cards
Lunch and dinner
Reservations required
Jacket required
Liquor served
Dinner: $25
   full 3 courses, without wine
Chef: Avrum Wiseman
Owners: Raymond and Dorothy Cosgrove

The RiverHouse on the Quay has a view of the magnificent Navesink River and its environs. Viewed from across the river are the verdant Highland hills, the highest point on the East Coast, and the historic Twin Lights lighthouses (atop the Highlands), beacons that once guided sailors into the harbor of New York City. In the summer it is pleasant to watch the never-ending parade of pleasurecraft that ply the waters outside the restaurant.

The recently built RiverHouse is situated on a strip of land between the Atlantic Ocean and the Navesink River. Decorated in muted shades of peach and blue, the restaurant seats 156. Because of the generous use of glass in the architecture of the building, there is a striking river view from every table. The comfortable lounge, with rustic tiling throughout, has a welcoming fireplace to warm visitors during the chilly winter months.

The menu features lobster and veal specialties, and other fine examples of American cuisine. The wine list is excellent. RiverHouse is on the Top 100 Restaurant Wine List compiled by *Wine Spectator* magazine.

NEW YORK
ALEXANDRIA BAY

Voyageur Room

Pine Tree Point Resort
P.O. Box 68
Alexandria Bay
New York 13607
Telephone: 315–482–9911

All major credit cards
Breakfast, lunch, and dinner
Reservations recommended
Jacket not required
Liquor served
Dinner: $9 to $23
    full 3 courses, without wine
Lunch: $3.75 to $7.50
Chef: Ray Bartholomew
Proprietors: Therése T. Thompson,
    Richard S. Thompson, and
    Roland Graham Thompson

The view of the Thousand Islands seen from the dining rooms, called the Voyageur Room and the Captain's Table, remind one of the Oslo Fjord; the dining room is similar to the one at the Highlands Inn near Carmel, California; and the view of Boldt's Castle is something like a Rhine view, near Bingen and Oppenheim.

This lodge is situated on its own private peninsula, surrounded on three sides by the tideless St. Lawrence River in a spot of scenic grandeur. The Indians named the area *Monatoana,* which means "Garden of the Great Spirit."

As you sit at your table, looking at the islands of the St. Lawrence, you are particularly impressed by the view of Heart Island, so named for its shape, and the beautiful Boldt's Castle you see on it. The castle's story is bittersweet. George C. Boldt spent $2.5 million building this castle, which he never finished, as a monument to (and summer home for) a great love, his wife. He started construction in 1895 but when his wife died in 1903 all work was stopped. The only parts of the structure that had been completed were the castle's shell, a power house, an Arch entrance, and the Alster Tower, which the Boldts used as a summer home while work was progressing.

Boldt's fascination with castles started as a poor boy in Prussia. He often saw castles along the Rhine and dreamed that he would someday have a castle of his own. Both the large castle, which we see from the Voyageur Room, and the smaller "playhouse," or Alster Tower, were modeled after Rhine castles. Boldt came to America and became the greatest hotel mogul of his day, owning the Waldorf-Astoria in New York and the Bellevue Stratford of Philadelphia. He died a multimillionaire.

There's more history to contemplate while dining—that of the St. Lawrence, which has been the scene of many important developments in U.S.-Canadian relations. For instance, the waters you look upon were the center of activity of Bill Johnston, who burned the British steamer *Sir Robert Peel* in an attempt to free Canada from British rule. Both British and Americans tried to capture this "pirate," as they called him, but he knew the Thousand Islands so well that he was able to avoid being caught.

Capt. C.S. Thompson bought the original site of the resort in 1911, sold it a while later, and bought it again in 1953, developing it as a resort. He further enlarged it in 1960, after a fire. He and his son, Andrew Graham Thompson, made it into a popular and successful resort. "Cap" passed away in 1967; Andrew died in 1969. The hotel is currently owned by Andrew's widow, Thérése; her sons Richard and Ronald help her run the operation. The dining room has been expanded to seat 235, while a newer dining room, the Captain's Table, seats 85. New, too, is a Sunday brunch featuring a six-course meal. There is also a Terrace Luncheon Sandwich Buffet, started last year; the terrace is the only place in the area where you can dine directly on the water with a view of Boldt's Castle.

The menu has been enlarged, offering appetizers ranging from Fresh Fruit Cup to Breaded Mushrooms. Entrées offer six selections of beef, four of veal, and various assortments of pork chops, chicken, and duck. There are eleven seafoods, ranging from Crabmeat Dewey (Alaskan King Crab in a cream-mushroom sauce laced with brandy and topped with Swiss cheese), to Maine Rock Lobster Tails.

A large salad bar, all of whose salad dressings are made in the Pine Tree Point kitchen, features, of course, Thousand Islands salad dressing.

BOLTON LANDING

Trillium

The Sagamore Hotel
  on Lake George
Bolton Landing
New York 12814
Telephone: 800-648-4901

All major credit cards
Reservations required
Jacket and tie required
Lunch: Monday through Friday; dinner: daily
Liquor served
Dinner: $26 to $35
  full 3 courses, without wine
Lunch: $12 to $15

The view to dine by here includes the rolling mountains of the Adirondacks and the sparkling freshwater Lake George. The Sagamore is a private island resort set on this lovely upstate New York lake.

This magnificently restored historic main hotel is surrounded by clusters of private cottages. The resort's top restaurant is called Trillium, named after a glorious light rose-colored lily which stands out as a solitary flower among a whirl of three leaves.

Dining here is supposed to bring the diner back in time to the resort's turn-of-the-century heyday, enabling guests to savor seasonal fare and chef specialties along with elaborate dishes offered more than 100 years ago. Dr. Lorna J. Sass, in her role as culinary historian, was commissioned to research and prepare a menu to include recipes of the late 19th century. The results are delightful.

Luncheon guests are offered *Pâté Maison* with Pear Cumberland Sauce, Jellied Borscht, Mallard Duck Salad with Warm Raspberry Vinaigrette, and Sole Sagamore, a poached sole with Lobster Ragout and White Wine Butter Sauce.

Among the dinner offerings are Partridge Camelia in Armagnac, Raisins, Port Wine, and Cream, Atlantic Salmon baked in Parchment with Mushrooms, Zucchini, and Fine Herbs, Maine Lobster with Cucumbers and Fresh Mint, and Gulf Snapper poached with Scallops and Shrimp. The appetizers, soups, and salads are just as varied: Lobster and Truffle Ravioli, Snails Trillium wrapped in Spinach, Phyllo Dough, and Fresh Tomato, Adirondack Fish Chowder, Asparagus and Truffle Salad, and a special Trillium Salad—a beautiful combination of Sea Scallops, Green Beans, and Caviar sprinkled with Basil Vinaigrette.

The Trillium flower appears in more than 20 shades of rose and pink and is resplendent on delicate linens, crystal, and fine Lilien Bellevue Austrian china designed for the Sagamore.

With such food to choose from one would think the view might play second fiddle. Well, .t's hard to say which is more spectacular. The Trillium is a peninsula of windows surrounded by exterior verandas overlooking scenic Lake George. The center of the dining room is raised so that nearly every guest is able to enjoy the view of the lake and the towering Adirondacks.

BROOKLYN

The River Café

1 Water Street
Brooklyn
New York 11201
Telephone: 718–522–5200

American Express, Diners Club
Lunch and dinner
Reservations necessary
Jacket required
Liquor served
Dinner: $45
    full 3 courses, without wine
Lunch: $12 to $19
Chef: Charles Palmer
Maitre d': N. Azzolini and J. Collison

The view from the River Café is simply stunning. You see the Brooklyn Bridge, the Wall Street area, the Statue of Liberty, the World Trade Center, the Woolworth building, and that's not all.

The view at night inside the restaurant is impressive, too. A pinstripe of light illuminates a beautiful floral arrangement on each table. The soft lighting creates a subtle ambience that permits celebrities to dine almost unnoticed. It is not unusual for Robert Redford, Frank Sinatra, John Huston, Mary Tyler Moore, or Elizabeth Taylor to be seated in this restaurant, sometimes at the same time. Heads of state, including the late Princess Grace of Monaco, Princess Margaret, the King and Queen of Sweden, and Queen Juliana of the Netherlands, have dined here.

The River Café is actually a coffee and spice barge dating from the 1940's. In 1977, it was positioned on an underwater pier in the East River and refitted with six-foot high windows spanning the length of the 90-foot barge. The owner, Michael O'Keefe, traveled extensively to provide many unusual decorating touches. The rattan chairs were made in Paris; the cobblestones on the driveway are from England; the oak floor is Australian; and

River Café

the extruded steel porch doors are from Belgium. Mr. O'Keefe tells us that this is the most photographed restaurant in America because of its intrinsic excitement. He says that guests of any age often stand in awe when they see the panorama of New York City on a crisp, clear night. He claims that it is probably for this reason that more people are proposed to at the River Café than at any other restaurant. While not provable, this is certainly believable.

The cuisine is exceptional and, in some instances, extraordinary. The chef specializes in unique domestic products, such as fresh buffalo, Muscovy and Mallard ducks, and seasonal game. The cuisine might be called refined American cooking.

Easy to find, the River Café is located on the East River, under the Brooklyn Bridge, on the Brooklyn side.

NEW YORK

Devereux's

The Essex House
160 Central Park South
New York
New York 10019
Telephone: 212-247-0300 Ext. 136

All major credit cards
Breakfast, lunch, dinner, and Sunday brunch
Reservations suggested
Jacket required
Liquor served
Dinner: $23 to $40
full 3 courses, without wine
Lunch: $15 to $25
Chef: Uwe Toedter

Seated at a window table in Devereux's Restaurant at the Essex House, you can gaze out on Central Park South and be fascinated by the contrasting metropolitan sights: the changing seasonal beauty of Central Park; horse-drawn carriages making their way through honking taxis and a stream of limousines; a steady flow of joggers and walkers in an amazing range of clothing. It's a scene that is uniquely New York City, and at the same time, it's a kaleidoscopic view of the peoples of the world. This is the ultimate people-watching vantage point.

Devereux's, at New York City's landmark Essex House, is characterized by roomy comfort, understated elegance, and a full-length view of Central Park and 59th Street. With a decor featuring shades of dusty pink, Devereux's has pastel fabric-covered walls, embroidered seat covers, burgundy patterned carpet, a pink marble floor, and mirrored walls. The color scheme is enhanced by crystal chandeliers and sconces, Oriental-style ceramic and brass urns filled with leafy plants, baskets of straw flowers, and a collection of Victorian-style paintings that includes one of Robert Devereux, the Earl of Essex.

The restaurant is divided into three sections so as to foster privacy. The elevated middle section is enclosed within banquettes mounted with etched-glass dividers in brass settings. The sunken area is distinguished by its fine wood paneling.

Prior to his arrival at Essex House, Executive Chef Toedter earned a reputation as one of the East Coast's most creative chefs while serving at the Vista International in Washington, D.C. He also conducted classes for students interested in the field of gastronomy. Toedter, a native of Hamburg, West Germany, has also been associated with a number of prestigious hotels and restaurants in Europe.

The cuisine features seafood and beef. Sunday brunch is served.

During the evening the view is a blur of lights, but one of fascinating movement; it is accompanied by a pianist playing softly to enhance the gracious dining.

Devereux's

Edwardian Room

in the Plaza
Fifth Avenue at Fifty-Ninth Street
New York
New York 10019
Telephone: 212-759-3000

All major credit cards
Breakfast, lunch, and dinner
Reservations necessary
Jacket required
Liquor served
Dinner: $40 to $55
full 3 courses, without wine
Lunch: $20 to $35
Chef: Reiner Greubal
Maitre d': Paul Nicaj

The view to dine by from the Edwardian Room is a privileged one. There are only a few tables situated by the high windows overlooking either Central Park or the plaza in front of the hotel's entrance, but the good news is that by asking for them well in advance you can usually get one with a view to dine by.

The view to the north, of Central Park, is nice but not the best. We prefer the view looking east, toward the General Motors skyscraper and Fifth Avenue. The bustling scene of horse-drawn carriages and well-dressed passersby is an animated and interesting one, and the little park between the hotel and Fifth Avenue is especially stimulating.

Its centerpiece is a large pedestal holding the equestrian statue of General Sherman done by Augustus Saint Gaudens. The piece won a gold medal at the Paris Salon in 1899. A statue of Pomona, goddess of Abundance, created by Karl Bitter, is also on the pedestal. Both statues rise above a fountain, around which is a favorite lunchtime spot for workers in the nearby buildings. This view was created as the result of a $50,000 bequest by Joseph Pulitzer to create a fountain in this mini plaza/park, which had had only General Sherman and some trees there since 1903. What you see was created in 1913. In 1923 the space was officially named Grand Army Plaza, in honor of the Union army of the Civil War.

Competing with the view is the decor and design of the Edwardian Room itself. When New York's Plaza Hotel opened its doors on October 1, 1907, advertised as "The World's Most Luxurious Hotel," it did not have the Edwardian Room. Nor did the space have a name; its patrons called it the Fifth Avenue Café. In 1955 it was formally named the Edwardian Room. For a brief time in the early 1970's it was changed to try to capture the mood of other trendy places in town; fortunately, good sense prevailed and its days as the "Green Tulip" will soon be forgotten, if they haven't been already. In 1974 the Edwardian Room was restored as the grand and elegant place it was and probably always will be.

The Edwardian Room was originally intended to provide the atmosphere of a private club for men only, a place where gentlemen could relax and enjoy masculine company, free from feminine "distractions." In the early days, certain unwritten rules were observed, as in private clubs. One of them prohibited the discussion of business; if one wanted to do that, he had to go to the famous bar in the back of the hotel (which came to be called the Oak Bar when it was reopened after prohibition and after E.F. Hutton and Company, which had occupied the space during prohibition, moved upstairs).

The view to dine by has changed over the years. In 1928, what had been the Vanderbilt mansion on the south side of "the plaza" was torn down to make way for the Bergdorf Goodman store, which is still there. Across Fifth Avenue, to the east, was the Hotel Savoy, which was also torn down in 1928, to be replaced by a more magnificent Savoy-Plaza Hotel. That too is gone, replaced in 1968 by the General Motors building designed by Edward Durrell Stone. In our opinion, Mr. Stone must never have dined in the Edwardian Room or he would not have designed such a bland, massive wall of a building.

Dining in the Edwardian Room, for any meal, is a special treat. When Westin Hotels bought the hotel in 1975, they resolved to keep the Plaza the fine hotel that it had been through the years. The Plaza is still one of New York's most beautiful sights, a designated landmark both by the city of New York and the National Register of Historic Places. So the superb cuisine of the Edwardian Room remains.

Among the dining room's specialties are Glazed Salmon Mornay with Mustard Seed, omelets made table-side, and Veal Paillard in Basil Sauce. All the desserts, including the gorgeous pastries, are made in the Plaza's bakery. All are wonderful.

Lutèce

249 East 50th Street
New York
New York 10022
212–752–2225/6

American Express, Diners Club, Carte Blanche
Lunch and dinner
Reservations recommended
Jacket and tie required
Liquor served
Dinner: $55
  full 3 courses, without wine
Lunch: $29 fixed price
Chef/owner: André Soltner

Frankly, although very pretty and enjoyable, the view to dine by at Lutèce is a modest one. It is to be had in the lovely skylighted garden room at the rear of this grandest of grand restaurants, where the sound of birds chirping (actually a recording) lends a nice touch to the proceedings.

The view may be modest, but the cuisine is not. Lutèce is said by many to be the finest restaurant in New York City. Since 1980, *Playboy* magazine, in its annual survey of the 25 best restaurants in the United States, has put Lutèce in first place three times. It is the efforts of the famed André Soltner and his wife, Simone, that make this restaurant so delightful and earn it so many awards. A full page of this book would be needed to list all of the culinary awards Soltner has received since he was an apprentice in Mulhouse in 1951. The 120-seat Lutèce, whose name comes from the old Roman name for the city of Paris, *Lutetia,* has been open since 1961.

Soltner's 20,000-bottle wine cellar is one of the restaurant's high points, but what contributes most to the charm and greatness of the Soltner dining room is that it embraces you with warmth rather than overwhelming you with too much service, too much decor, or too much food.

Quality is the obvious and understated concern, ranging from pâtés to pastries, from the zinc bar to the garden room, from the elegant linen to the tasteful silver place settings. You can scan the menu yourself, but many diners seem to prefer a careful consultation with the chef/owner himself. Among the specialties he might recommend are a simple roast chicken, *Medaillons de Veau,* and *Saumon en Croute.* The desserts, too, are tantalizing; we suggest you try the *Soufflé Glace.*

The more affluent of New York's big business and high society world congregate at Lutèce. Located in a small townhouse in the center of Manhattan, it has a staff of 16 in the kitchen. André spends about three-quarters of his time in the kitchen while his wife, Simone, takes care of the front of the house.

Is the cuisine French, international, or American? André says that he runs this restaurant as if it were in Paris, but he is reluctant to give a nationalistic label to his food. "French cuisine is good because France is blessed with wonderful food, with wonderful ingredients with which to start. America is the same. I've been here about 25 years. Italian, Chinese, Spanish, French, this is all American food here. I believe in only one cuisine— good cuisine."

Riveranda and Empress of New York

Pier 62
West 23rd Street and
  the Hudson River
New York
New York 10011
Telephone: 212–929–7090

All major credit cards
Dinner and Sunday brunch
Reservations required
Jacket requested
Liquor served
Dinner: $40 to $45
  full 3 courses,
  without wine
Lunch: $22 to $25
Chef: Bruce Sacino

At last, New York can compete with the Paris *Bateaux Mouches* on the Seine and other dinner ships around the world. In fact, according to articles that have appeared in *Gourmet, Travel & Leisure,* and other publications, New York's dinner cuisine is the best of them all.

New York's first and only (at the moment) restaurant yachts are the Riveranda and the Empress of New York. You may stroll on the promenade decks, relax with a cocktail, and then dine on freshly prepared and beautifully served selections from the on-board galleys. And all the while you will have a view to dine by of the incomparable Manhattan skyline and its dramatic, continuously changing vistas, as the restaurant yacht sails through New York's harbors and waterways. In addition to an international cuisine offering a wide choice of salads, appetizers, hot and cold entrées, fresh vegetables, and fine desserts, music, dancing, and entertainment are offered. Fully enclosed, the dining room offers the meals and views year-round.

The Empress seats 375 at dinner and the Riveranda seats 275; both took their first dinner voyage on July 30, 1984. The Empress is a luxuriously converted U.S. Navy ship that crossed the Atlantic during World War II; the Riveranda is a vessel designed and built to be a cruising restaurant.

The ships normally leave at 7 P.M., but guests often arrive early, mainly to get window tables; don't worry, though, if you can't arrive early—all seats have views.

Operated by a company called World Yacht Enterprises, the Empress and the Riveranda travel some thirty miles of waterways around the island of Manhattan. It is a refreshing journey, particularly on a nice day or on a sunset cruise. On Thursdays to Saturdays there is a pre-theater cruise from 4:30 P.M. until 6:30 P.M. and there is a starlight cruise from 9 P.M. until midnight. Most popular is the 7 P.M. cruise. The weekday lunch cruises are from 11:30 A.M. until 1:30 P.M., and the Sunday brunch cruises start at 12:30 P.M. and return at 2:30 P.M. There are midnight cruises at which only hors d'oeuvres and drinks are served.

The Sea Grill

Rockefeller Plaza
19 West 49th Street
New York
New York 10020
Telephone: 212–246–9201

All major credit cards
Lunch and dinner
Reservations necessary
Jacket required
Liquor served
Dinner: $35
  full 3 courses, without wine
Lunch: $16 to $24
Chef: Konstantin Schonbachler
Maitre d': Peter Wyss

The Sea Grill is a new restaurant (opened in 1984) in the heart of Rockefeller Plaza. In the summer and spring, its side is opened and the restaurant is expanded to provide outdoor dining in a flower-filled garden setting. This "garden" is set up every spring in the area which in winter becomes an ice-skating rink, and thus a different view to dine by. At Christmastime, the view also encompasses the famous gigantic Rockefeller Center Christmas tree. The golden Prometheus Fountain by Paul Manship can be seen year-round (though the fountains do not run in winter).

The Sea Grill itself has a delightful decor designed to conjure up the sea. The North Light bounces in the windows on Rockefeller Plaza, moonlight flows down through the glass-bottomed pools set in the ceiling, and light filters through the bottles of garnet and amber wines, making them look like stained glass windows. Soft wools in the colors of the seashore carpet the floor.

The deep armchairs are modeled after those welcoming first-class passengers on transatlantic liners. A ruddy cherrywood is used on the ceiling, in the columns and arches, and on the walls. Below the pools in the ceiling, a second pair of pools add the sparkle and murmur of cascading water to the room.

The kitchen is visible, set behind chilled marble counters where the day's catch, herbs and vegetables, and pastries are all displayed.

Regional dishes featuring native finfish and shellfish are prominent on the menu, served grilled over hardwood coals and grapevines in the light and exquisite West Coast-style and in simple raw-bar style. Maine Lobsters weighing from two-and-a-half to three pounds are served steamed, poached, or grilled. Breast of Pheasant, Calf's Liver, veal, and steak are grilled, too. All of the desserts, including ice creams and fruit ices, are made in the Sea Grill pastry shop.

The Sun Garden and
The Crystal Fountain

of the Grand Hyatt New York
Park Avenue at Grand Central Station
New York
New York 10017
Telephone: 212–883–1234

All major credit cards
Breakfast, lunch, and dinner
Reservations not necessary
Dress: casual but neat
Liquor served
Dinner: $16 to $35
  full 3 courses, without wine
Lunch: $8 to $16
Chef: Helmut Leuck

The Grand Hyatt opened in 1980 as a modern showpiece in the heart of New York City. Its architecture is a delightful interplay of space, marble, water, and glass.

The hotel is a 34-story glass edifice which reflects the historic architecture of its neighbors, including the famous art deco skyscraper, the Chrysler building. The Grand Hyatt has a dramatic waterfall cascading over a marble wall in its three-level entryway. The lobby has fashionable boutiques and attractive restaurants with views.

The Crystal Fountain is the name given to the 365-seat restaurant on the lobby level. Here tables surround the fountain from which the restaurant takes its name. The huge floor-to-ceiling windows that flood the restaurant with natural light provide diners with a dramatic view of the landmark Chrysler building across the street. The Crystal Fountain features an open bakery and serves food far superior to that of the average hotel.

Overlooking the rush and hubbub of midtown Manhattan's 42nd Street is the Sun Garden cocktail lounge, a lush, plant-filled greenhouse actually cantilevered over the sidewalk. The Sun Garden is an ideal place to have lunch or cocktails while watching the endless march of people below, many of whom are going into or coming from Grand Central Station, located next door. This is one of the few spots where rain or snow enhances the dining atmosphere. There's also a view of the waterfall in the atrium. In the evening, guests enjoy refreshments under the stars while listening to a string trio perform.

Tavern on the Green

in Central Park
at Central Park West and 67th Street
New York
New York 10023
Telephone: 212–873–3200

All major credit cards
Lunch and dinner
Reservations recommended
Liquor served
Dinner $9.50 to $21.50
 full 3 courses, without wine
Lunch: $8.50 to $19.50
Chef: Reto Demarmels
Pastry Chef: Dieter Schoener

The Tavern on the Green is situated in New York City's Central Park, on city-owned space rented to Warner LeRoy, the restaurateur who also created Maxwell's Plum.

The view of the park is unquestionably beautiful, encompassing trees and lawns, horse-drawn carriages, equestrians, joggers, and other staples of New York City life. The view inside is equally impressive: huge reflective chandeliers and twinkling lights wherever you look. The atmosphere is so festive that this is certainly one of the city's most popular places for celebrations and parties of all sorts, although couples, too, find it a romantic and even private spot to be.

Among the recommended main dishes are Red Snapper with Julienned Sweet Vegetables, Rib Roast, Green Pasta Dressed with Chicken, Mushrooms, and Cream, and Tagliorini (fine egg pasta) with Scallops, Sole, Basil, Tomato, and Cooked Vegetables. The desserts are colorful and, if you're watching your weight, downright sinful.

Top of the Park
One Gulf & Western Plaza
60th and Central Park West
New York
New York 10023
Telephone: 212-333-3800

All major credit cards
Dinner
Reservations recommended
Jacket required
Liquor served
Dinner: $19.50 to $27.50
    full 3 courses, without wine
Chef: Alain de Coster
Maitre d': Andre Fevrier

In 1970, when Gulf & Western built this skyscraper overlooking Central Park, Stuart Levin, the owner of a famous New York French restaurant, Le Pavillon, was asked to create a dining room on the roof of the building. Both a private dining room for executive luncheons and a stylish rooftop dinner spot for a sophisticated clientele were requested.

Levin agreed, but with the understanding that he could set it up not as a tourist attraction, but rather as an elegant dining room serving, for the most part, the residents living in the luxury condominium and cooperative apartments nearby, all having magnificent views of their own of the broad expanse of beautiful Central Park.

Levin knew that the restful view was really nothing new to most of his guests, so he designed a dining room with beauty and charm. Levin has just completed a full remodeling, changing the decor after 15 years. A rich brown, red, and black carpet has replaced the royal blue and red one of old. The table lights have been changed from red to crystallized glass, and all the walls are mirrored, adding light and providing a fuller panoramic view of the city. The dining room seats 120 and is 43 floors above Central Park.

As you enter the reception area you can see the sparkling New Jersey skyline. In the center of this panorama is the brightly lighted Meadowlands sports complex. And the Hudson River seems dramatically dark and close, even though it isn't.

Walking to the dining room on the opposite side of the bar in the reception area, you look right down into Central Park and over to Fifth Avenue, on the other side of the park. This spectacular view is visible from any table and gets better as it gets darker.

The food competes with the view. Alain de Coster has earned recognition in all the guidebooks for his international cuisine. One favorite is Rack of Lamb; others include the Tournedo of Beef and Roast Duckling with Peaches. Among the tantalizing desserts, we suggest the Frozen Sand Pie, which is made with coffee ice cream, crushed Italian cookies (called amaretti), and crushed coffee beans which are placed in a graham cracker mold, frozen, and then served with hot chocolate sauce and whipped cream. Because the meal portions are so generous you might be tempted to skip dessert. Don't skip this one.

The View
New York
Marriott
Marquis

1535 Broadway
New York
New York 10036
Telephone: 212–398–190

All major credit cards
Lunch and dinner
Reservations necessary
Jacket required
Liquor served
Chef: Willy Ribbe

Photo courtesy of John Woodward

In October 1985, the 1,877-room New York Marriott Marquis hotel opened its doors in Times Square, the heart of New York City. This is a hotel of superlatives: it has the largest hotel atrium in the world, it is the largest—at 50 stories—of the Marriott hotels, and it is the first building to go up as part of a major effort to restore Times Square's badly tarnished luster. The hotel's arrival has begun to inspire others to contribute to the upgrading and beautification of the world-renowned center of America's largest international city.

Most exciting to us is the area of the hotel on its 46th through 48th floor, where there is a three-level revolving restaurant complex. Although there are revolving restaurants all around the world, this is the first of its kind in Manhattan. On clear days one can see three states (New York, New Jersey, and Connecticut) and four bodies of water—the Atlantic Ocean, Long Island Sound, and the Hudson and East Rivers.

You enter from a special elevator from the ninth level of the hotel, which carries the restaurant guests up through the immense atrium, past skylights and ivy-covered internal terraces to the 46th floor. The View seats 196 and offers an international menu. Opened in December 1985, it is furnished in dark, rich fabrics, accented by sparkling brass.

Above the restaurant is the View Lounge, which seats 505 guests comfortably. It has the same spectacular revolving view and is destined to become the spot for New York's sophisticated set to enjoy cocktails while watching the sun set.

The New York Marriott Marquis is the newest luxury hotel in New York City. Its history started in 1972 when Mayor John Lindsay approached the Atlanta-based architect and developer John Portman with an idea. The Mayor envisioned a larger-than-life hotel on an 85,000 square-foot Times Square site that could accommodate the growing influx of visitors and conventioneers to New York City. Portman, an innovator whose efforts led to the building of the first floor-to-ceiling atrium hotel, the Atlanta Hyatt Regency, in the 1960s, said he was ready to accept the challenge.

A challenge it was. There were problems with financing and conservationists, as well as debates over air rights. Eventually, Mayor Ed Koch and his administrative associates gave Portman the collaboration he needed. A partnership was eventually formed involving Marriott and Portman, and the project, originally planned to cost $170 million, was started.

Now, more than a decade after it was conceived, the New York Marriott Marquis (which ended up costing some $450 million) is a major Times Square attraction. The hotel has its own 1,500-seat Broadway theater, 141 exquisite and luxurious suites, glass elevators gliding through a 46-story atrium, the largest grand ballroom in New York City, which can accommodate up to 3,500 guests, four lounges and four world-class restaurants under the direction of executive chef Willy Ribbe, who has been an executive chef for 18 years in six different countries.

Windows on the World

107th floor
One World Trade Center
New York
New York 10048–0605
Telephone: 212–938–1111

All major credit cards
Breakfast, lunch, dinner,
  and Sunday brunch
Reservations recommended
Restaurant: jacket and tie required
Hors d'Oeuvrerie: jacket required
Liquor served
Restaurant:
  Dinner: $29.95 prix fixe,
  without wine
  À la carte: entrées $17.50 to $23
  Hors d'Oeuvrerie:
  Breakfast: $3.95 to $12;
  other meals, hot/cold
  $4.95 to $9.50
Chef: Hermann Reiner
Maitre d': Lee Harty

Unless you are eating in an airplane, or in heaven, the highest view to dine by in the world is the aptly named Windows on the World, on the 107th floor of the World Trade Center in the financial district of New York City. The view is truly startling; in fact, some people have trouble getting used to it. It is not as high as the view from an airplane, but it sure seems that way. It is actually better than an airplane view because you see it, leisurely, from an elegantly set table through large windows, rather than stretching to catch a fleeting glimpse of a swiftly passing panorama.

Even when the weather is not clear enough to secure the 55-mile visibility you get on a clear day, the view is enough to make poets of ordinary people. One patron seated next to us said, when lightning flashed, "It's so beautiful that God took a flash picture." Another saw the Queen Elizabeth II float ethereally from the Hudson River into a fog-covered Atlantic Ocean and called it a movie dream sequence. Another sour-faced guest was silent as he took in all of the views of Manhattan and beyond and said, "It goes to show you that even the ugly is beautiful if you just step back and take a long look."

Philosophers, dreamers, and ordinary sightseers, too, find the view a grand experience whether it is a first or fiftieth visit. You can see Manhattan, Brooklyn, Long Island, and much of Northern New Jersey. The Statue of Liberty, the Empire State Building, the green expanse of Central Park, and the 747s rising from and landing at John F. Kennedy International Airport—these are the elements of your view to dine by.

Not only do many New Yorkers bring their out-of-town and foreign visitors here to see New York City from its most beautiful vantage point, but they bring their families, too, particularly for Sunday brunch. Windows on the World is truly an international dining spot, for whenever we have been here, the languages spoken by the diners made it seem as if the United Nations general assembly had adjourned to dine here.

Upon contemplating this scene, you are also moved to ask a somewhat intriguing question: did the founders of New York City—the Dutch, the English, and then the Americans—ever imagine that their small city would reach such huge dimensions in so many ways? The men that built the nearby historic landmarks, such as the stock exchanges, Trinity Church, the Wall Street office buildings, Federal Hall (where George Washington was inaugurated as president), the original South Street Seaport, and City Hall, would probably never believe that their work would be looked down upon from a dining room some 1,350 feet (412 meters) above!

Windows on the World is actually a collection of dining rooms. The largest is simply

Windows on the World

called The Restaurant and has the best views from all of its 350 seats. Despite its size, it is cozy and intimate because it is sectioned off and terraced so everyone can see everything. It offers a truly international cuisine, representative of the makeup of its guests. It is open for dinner Monday through Saturday from 5 P.M. until 10 P.M., on Saturday from noon until 2:30 P.M. for brunch, and on Sunday from noon until 7:30 P.M. Lunch is served Monday through Friday from noon until 2:15 P.M., when The Restaurant is a private club mostly for occupants of the World Trade Center buildings. Nonmembers are charged a $7.50 cover charge at lunch only, but for an annual fee anyone can join. In the center of The Restaurant is the Grand Buffet Table, where pastries are temptingly displayed at dinnertime, and where the Grand Buffet is displayed for Saturday luncheon and all day Sunday.

The menu of The Restaurant features charcoal-grilled meats, the special Rack of Lamb James Beard, and what the menu describes as "always the freshest oysters around." The desserts offer such treats as Chocolate Sabayon Cake, luscious White Chocolate Mousse, and Warm Apple Tart. The staff in this room speaks 11 languages.

The Hors d'Oeuvrerie is smaller, but not small, with 240 seats, and bills itself as "America's first international hors d'oeuvre restaurant." It is designed to look like a dinner theater, with tiered seating to provide a view of the open kitchen—the International Cooks' Table—as the stage. Cooks in colorful national dress prepare and serve their countries' regional specialties. From a selection of over 20 hot and cold hors d'oeuvres such as sushi, sashimi, Moroccan kefta, Indonesian sates, Kyoto beef roll, coconut fried shrimp, and Szechuan hacked chicken, you can put together an entire meal. The Hors d'Oeuvrerie also contains the City Lights Bar.

It is open at 7:30 A.M. on weekdays for breakfast and the rising sun. At 3 P.M. the bar opens and samples of the hors d'oeuvres are served. The piano begins at 4:30 P.M. and a trio takes over at 7:30 P.M. and plays until 1 A.M. Tuesday through Saturday (12:30 A.M. on Mondays). On Sunday tea dancing begins at 4 P.M. There is a $2.75 cover charge whenever there is dance music. Sunday brunch is served from noon until 3 P.M. Jackets are required and denims are not permitted. The Hors D'Oeuvrerie also offers views of Manhattan and beyond.

There is a restaurant here which has no view because it is in the heart of the Windows on the World complex; called the Cellar in the Sky, it is a small romantic dining room which seats only 36. This really isn't a restaurant; rather, it is the working wine cellar for the complex, so the guests are surrounded by thousands of bottles of wine. Dappled lights reflect the wine's ambers and reds on the cool marble floor, so there is a view of sorts. This room has a special gourmet menu for its limited guests with a prix fixe of $70 a person. Reservations are necessary.

Windows on the World is an operation of Inhilco, Inc., a wholly owned subsidiary of Hilton International. Anton Aigner is the president of Inhilco, which is responsible for serving 25,000 to 30,000 guests every day at Windows on the World. The vice-president, director, and host is Alan Lewis, who calls Windows "the biggest neighborhood restaurant in the world."

NORTH CAROLINA
MAGGIE VALLEY
The Cataloochee Ranch

Route 1
Maggie Valley
North Carolina 28751
Telephone: 704–926–1401

All major credit cards
Breakfast, lunch, and dinner
Reservations required for non-guests
Dress: informal
Dinner: $11 to $15
    full 3 courses, without wine
Lunch: $4 to $7
Managing Partner: Alice A. Aumen

The views from the mile-high surroundings here are spectacular. Most people consider the Balsam Mountain Range of the Great Smokies to be the primary view (to the east and south), but the northern view, of the Great Smoky Mountain National Park and the grazing meadows for the cattle and ranch horses, is magnificent, too. Included in this view is the trout pond where guests of the ranch may catch their own breakfast or lunch; later they can look out over the pond from the dining room while enjoying their trout.

The dining room is in the ranch house itself, which is a recently (1982) remodeled stone and log barn. During 1986-87 the dining, public, and kitchen areas will be completely redone. The new dining room, like its predecessor, will be filled with antiques and hand-crafted furniture. The dining tables are solid cherry wood. Centerpieces with freshly arranged wildflowers from the surrounding woods and meadows are used. Several times a week, lunch or dinner may be served on the terrace just outside the dining room, making the diner feel more a part of the majestic view.

The new dining room will reflect the same refined, rustic informality that the old one did. Because of the cool climate, the fireplaces will be lighted most of the time.

At dinnertime usually one or two meat dishes are offered. Occasionally outdoor meals like trout fries or steak cookouts are organized. But dinner is generally served in the dining room. Salads and vegetables in large quantities, such as Zucchini Creole and Fresh Steamed and Buttered Snow Peas, as well as homemade breads and great desserts like Chocolate Upside Down Cake and fruit cobblers are featured.

Because appetites are stimulated by the fresh mountain air, generous portions are always served. And although until recently only guests of the ranch could be served in the dining room, now visitors and residents in the area are welcome so long as they make reservations, particularly for breakfast and dinner.

PENNSYLVANIA
BOILING SPRINGS
The Carriage Room

at Allenberry "on the Yellow Breeches"
Resort Inn
Route 174
Box 7
Boiling Springs
Pennsylvania 17007
Telephone: 717–258–3211

All major credit cards
Dinner
Reservations recommended
Jacket not required
Liquor served
Dinner: $11 to $18
    full 3 courses, without wine
Chef: Danial Raudabaugh

This fine dining room is located on the same resort property as Fairfield Hall (see next entry), but its dining room serves à la carte regional cuisine and it is known for its excellent food and fine self-service wine cellar, featuring a broad selection of Pennsylvania wines made in nearby wineries. The Carriage Room is in an addition built on the 1812 Stone Lodge.

It has a different view than Fairfield Hall, with large windows looking out on the shady maples and abundant rhododendrons planted around a charming brick patio and fern-encrusted limestone walls. Birds, chipmunks, squirrels, and ducks parade by for the entertainment of the diners. And here you hope for at least a chill wind, since that becomes an excuse to have a fire in the beautiful large stone fireplace at the end of the room.

The Carriage Room's menu is unique in the area. It offers such entrées as Broiled Rainbow Trout, Barbequed Baby Back Ribs, Cajun Redfish, Sautéed Veal with Mushrooms, Broiled Oysters with Lump Crab and Garlic, and Grilled Breast of Duck. They are served with soup, such as Danny's Seafood Chowder, salads including Marinated Artichoke Hearts, and hot garlic bread with brie and stilton cheeses. There are chilled summer soups and seasonal vegetables. Desserts include a hot fudge sundae served in a "Paul Bunyon"-sized champagne glass, chocolate/fresh fruit fondue, and homemade carrot cake.

Fairfield Hall

at Allenberry "on the Yellow Breeches"
Resort Inn
Route 174
Box 7
Boiling Springs
Pennsylvania 17007
Telephone: 717–258–3211

All major credit cards
Breakfast, lunch, and dinner
Reservations recommended
Jacket not required
Liquor served
Dinner buffet: $12.95
Lunch buffet: $8.25
Proprietor: The Heinze Family
  President: John J. Heinze
  Manager: Jere S. Heinze

Fairfield Hall was constructed around 1785 as a limestone dairy barn but has been made into a delightful place to dine. It is one of the largest remaining bank barns in central Pennsylvania, and is set in the hillside above the Yellow Breeches Creek. The creek was so named during the Revolutionary period when soldiers who waded or washed their white breeches in the waters found they turned yellow from the churning silt.

Looking south from the Hall, guests can see the creek, now one of the best trout fishing streams in America. Next to the creek is the small Still House; a guest house now, it was once the home of a distiller who made the grains of the large productive farm into a popular "cash" product. Also in the view is Mansion House, the private residence of Mrs. Mary Lu Heinze. Among its past owners was a relative of the folk hero, Davy Crockett. Mansion House became a farm in 1685, when the land was granted.

Fairfield Hall is open every day for breakfast and lunch. Buffet dinners are served Wednesday through Saturday. The buffet dinner consists of Country Ham, Roast Steamship of Beef, Roasted Chicken, Seafood Newburg, fresh vegetables and salads, fruits, cheeses, famous Pennsylvania Dutch Lebanon bologna, and their own delightful sticky buns and homemade ice cream. Fairfield Hall is located on Route 174, 20 miles southwest of Harrisburg.

RHODE ISLAND
NEWPORT

Le Bistro

Bowen's Wharf
Newport
Rhode Island 02840
Telephone: 401–849–7778

All major credit cards
Lunch and dinner
Reservations necessary
Jacket not required
Liquor served
Dinner: $18 to $38
  full 3 courses, without wine
Lunch: $9 to $22
Chef: John Philcox
Proprietors: John and Mary Philcox

Le Bistro is a delightful restaurant on the second and third floors of a semimodern building on Bowen's Wharf, at West Pelham Street in Newport. It is in an area busy with tourists and the sailors who frequent the wharf, but, located as it is above the activity, it is free of the hubbub.

From both floors one has beautiful views of the harbor, particularly delightful when the sun sets. The two dining rooms are on the second floor and each seats 50, while the bar on the floor above seats 20.

John and Mary Philcox are glad that visitors enjoy the view but they themselves concentrate on preparing fine cuisine. Dinner is served from 6 P.M. until 10 P.M., with about a dozen main courses and appetizers, plus the daily offerings of seafood. Everything is very fresh, purchased that day. In addition to a dinner menu, there is a simpler menu available in the bar all day and at lunch that includes sandwiches, salads, and some country-style entrées such as *Saucisson Chaud* and *Bouillabaisse*. The dining room has become known for its unusual specialties, such as sweetbreads and veal kidneys, and its own *pâtés* and *terrines*.

Special wines come from a neighbor, the Sakonnet Vineyards in Little Compton.

This dining room has received many complimentary reviews, has been called one of the best restaurants in New England by a number of critics, and has had its recipes featured in several magazines.

Newport is really two different towns. In summer, it is a very busy tourist city, with a regular summer colony and sightseers who come to see the mansion "cottages" built during the turn of the century by some of America's most wealthy families. During the rest of the year it is a small New England town with more restaurants than it really needs. Le Bistro is one of the few restaurants that requires guests to make reservations year-round.

TENNESSEE
KNOXVILLE

The Volador Room

Hyatt Regency Knoxville
500 Hill Avenue S.E.
Knoxville
Tennessee 37901
Telephone: 615–637–1234

All major credit cards
Dinner
Reservations recommended
Jacket required
Liquor served
Dinner: $15 to $20
    full 3 courses, without wine
Chef: Jim Higgins
Maitre d': John Shanks

Looking to the southeast from the Volador Room, toward the rolling East Tennessee Hills, overlooking the Tennessee River, one sees a breathtaking view of the main chain of the Great Smoky Mountains, climaxing with the peaks of Clingman's Dome and Mount LeConte.

It is so lovely here that the local people call the Volador Room of the Hyatt Regency Knoxville "the restaurant where the stars come out at night." This actually has two meanings. It refers, of course, to the great view, but it also means that the room is a favorite of local as well as national celebrities.

This is also a fun place. People are still talking about the time the waiters served a pig's head, with an ample cigar in its mouth, to the astonished mayor of Knoxville, who is, luckily, famous for his sense of humor. But the mayor's presence here was no surprise, since the Volador Room is the showplace of Knoxville. Opened in March 1972, this restaurant brought many new dining practices to town, including table-side service highlighted with flaming dishes and cordial and dessert carts, as well as an extensive presentation of soups, appetizers, exotic wines, and liqueurs.

The decor, featuring dark colors and soft lighting, produces a romantic atmosphere. The hotel itself is striking, with its atrium lobby and glass elevators which rise through the lobby and emerge on the exterior of the building, as they continue up to the top floor (the eleventh), where guests arrive at the Volador Room. So while riding in the elevator, you get a preview of the view to dine by.

TEXAS
DALLAS

Antares

Atop the Reunion Tower
Hyatt Regency Dallas
300 Reunion Boulevard
Dallas
Texas 75207
Telephone: 214–651–1234

All major credit cards
Lunch, dinner, and Sunday brunch
Reservations suggested
Jacket not required
Liquor served
Dinner: $20 to $28
    full 3 courses, without wine
Lunch: $5.50 to $7.50
Chef: Eddie Peyer
Manager: Norman Shiman

Antares

There's a lot of Dallas to see, and the best place to start is atop the 50-story Reunion Tower, where, in a revolving restaurant, you can get a 360-degree view of the city and its outskirts.

This is the best view of the area you can get, and it includes the popular amusement park, Six Flags Over Texas in nearby Arlington, the Arlington Stadium, home of the Texas Rangers, and the Fort Worth skyline to the south. You also see the Trinity River and the beautiful Green Belt, as well as the massive Dallas/Fort Worth Airport, which is larger than Manhattan Island. To the west, the Texas Stadium, home of the Dallas Cowboys, is visible, as well as the famous Dallas Market Center which includes the World Trade Center, the Apparel Mart, the Market Hall, the Home Furnishing Mart, the Decorative Center, and the Trade Mart. Also in view are Love Field, Southern Methodist University, and the 1891 Romanesque Old Red Courthouse (you can even see the gargoyles with a pair of binoculars). To the north is the John Neely Bryan Cabin, home of the Dallas settler who founded the city in 1841, the John Fitzgerald Kennedy Memorial designed by architect Philip Johnson, and the Dallas County Courthouse. In addition, toward the east you see the beautiful Dallas City Hall designed by architect I.M. Pei, the State Fair Park, with its Cotton Bowl Stadium, State Fair Music Hall, and the world's largest fair, the State Fair of Texas. Also to the east is the Old City Park, the Reunion Arena, and the Dallas Convention Center with an adjoining Memorial Auditorium.

The 50-story Reunion Tower has a unique geodesic dome, and it is the architectural landmark of Dallas. The three-level dome is studded with 240 light bulbs, creating a spectacular nighttime display. The dome weighs 50 tons, contains 114,000 separate parts, and uses over two miles of aluminum pipe. At 560 feet, its highest level is "At Top of the Dome," a revolving cocktail lounge that makes a complete turn every 55 minutes.

Antares, named for the brightest star in the Scorpio constellation, is the Continental restaurant at the dome's middle level. Guests are brought up to the restaurant in glass-enclosed elevators located in the tower's three outer concrete shafts.

The guests include out-of-town visitors, guests of the hotel, and local residents. One diner proposed to the young lady with whom he was dining by having an airplane fly by the window during dinner, trailing a sign that said "Will you marry me?"

Chicken in the Stars, half a young chicken with teriyaki marinade and fresh sautéed vegetables, is the recommended specialty at lunch. At dinner, a Texas favorite is, of course, Prime Ribs of Blue Ribbon Beef, a most tender serving of prize-winning beef along with fresh country vegetables. Other favorites include (at lunch) Tower Taco (the dining room's version of taco salad) and Reuben Pizza. At dinner, another popular dish is Seafood Teriyaki. The desserts include Double Chocolate Mousse and Profiteroles Zabaglione, tiny puffs filled with creamy custard set in cold zabaglione sauce, ribboned with hot bitterfudge sauce. At dinner you are served a *palette pacifier,* a cone of tart sherbet to refresh your taste buds between courses. Another dinner treat is a basket of grilled French herb bread.

Adjoining the modern Reunion Tower is the futuristic, 947-room Hyatt Regency Hotel, with its 18-story lobby, itself offering a view to dine by at Fausto's Sea Catch.

Laurel's

Sheraton Park Central Hotel
12720 Merit Drive
Dallas
Texas 75251
Telephone: 214–385–3000

All major credit cards
Dinner
Reservations recommended
Jacket and tie required
Liquor served
Dinner: $35 to $50
    full 3 courses, without wine
Chef: Tim Rodgers
Maitre d': Sal LaCayo

Laurel's is the only rooftop restaurant in North Dallas. The entire exterior wall of the restaurant is glass, providing diners with a full view of downtown Dallas and beyond. Local publications rave about the view, with the *Dallas Times Herald* calling it "magnificent" and *D* magazine labeling it "fabulous." The view has been credited as providing Laurel's with an ambience that makes it one of the most romantic restaurants in Dallas.

Both the hotel and the restaurant are new, having opened in 1983. Designed by Dallas architects Hellmuth, Obata, and Kassabaum, Inc., with interiors by Jutras and Nobill Associates of Bedford, Massachusetts, the Sheraton Park Central is a place of elegance and grace.

Its food is as fine as its view. The chef and chef artist have won awards for the beautiful presentation of the dishes served here. Among the more popular selections are Corn Velvet with Louisiana Lump Crab Meat, Steamed Salmon Fillet with Scallop Mousse and Seabean, Roast Loin of Lamb with Roasted Peppers and Southwest Salad, Symphony of Seafood on a Trio of Sauces, and Grilled *Poussin* with Fresh Pasta. The house-specialty accompaniment to most meals is the delicious molasses-nut bread. There's an after-dinner cordial cart offering diners a selection of exquisite liqueurs. For dessert, we recommend the fresh blueberries (in season) and whipped cream and the ricotta cheese/sponge cake.

FORT WORTH

The Old Swiss House

1541 Merrimac Circle
Fort Worth
Texas 76107
Telephone: 817–877–1531

All major credit cards
Dinner
Reservations advisable
Jacket encouraged
Liquor served
Dinner: $13 to $25
    full 3 courses, without wine
Chef/Owner: Walter F. Kaufmann
Maitre d': Pat Ragsdale (Ms.)

Fort Worth's first European-style restaurant also has the best view to dine by in the city. Diners seated at or near the high wall of windows overlook the scenic Trinity River. You can sometimes see the moon rising over the treetops and reflected in the tranquil river waters. Commenting on the view, the owner and chief chef, Walter F. Kaufmann, says that "all that's missing are the mountains; on a clear day, you can even see those."

When we first dined here, Chef Kaufmann, wearing his white outfit and chef's high hat, came to chat with us while we were enjoying our meal. "How wonderful," we thought, "he came out just to see us." Not so, we found out. Kaufmann talked to many other guests before returning to the kitchen. That's the kind of place this is. It is as if we are the chef's friends and are eating in his personal dining room.

For more than a decade, *Travel/Holiday* has listed this establishment in its *Guide to Fine Dining.* For more than two decades, Kaufmann and his wife Nancy have brought Continental cuisine at its best to Fort Worth. Kaufmann is responsible for introducing local restaurantgoers to such delicacies as *Escalopes de Veau "Oscar"* (veal sautéed in butter and topped with crabmeat and Hollandaise), *Filet Mignon Sauté King Henri IV, Carre d'Agneau Persillade* (rack of lamb with parsley, bread crumbs, and mustard), and others.

Asked what dishes his guests like, Walter told us that a favorite appetizer is cold cucumber soup, and the favorite main course is Poached Norwegian Salmon with Cucumber Sauce. Favorite desserts include Strawberries Walter and Cherries Jubilee.

Walter Kaufmann's cooking is special. When he uses herbs, sauces, and dressings, they are only employed to bring out the flavor of the meat, not to smother it. He feels that good meat and good seafood should be helped to preserve their natural flavor and not be so drowned in seasonings that they become unidentifiable.

HOUSTON

La Tour d'Argent

2011 Ella Boulevard
and T.C. Jester
Houston
Texas 77008
Telephone: 713-864-9864

All major credit cards
Lunch and dinner
Reservations necessary
Jacket required
Liquor served
Dinner: $28 to $32
    full 3 courses, without wine
Lunch: $13
Chef: Maurice Couturier
Maitre d's: Tony Vasquez and Mike Lahham

Quite a contrast from the original Tour d'Argent in Paris, this restaurant is called "The French Log Cabin," and it is indeed a log cabin, a beautiful one at that! The cuisine by Chef Couturier is very French, and earned the restaurant the coveted *Mobil* United States and Canada 1984 and 1985 Four Star Award for Outstanding Food Presentation, atmosphere, service, and extensive wine list.

This log cabin was built in the early 20th century by Alex Curpin, a French Canadian carpenter. It took him three years to build, using only a few simple tools—an ax, a hammer, an adz, and a saw. Logs of pine, oak, and cypress were used from the San Jacinto River bottom, along with a carload of Walker County stone for the fireplaces. In 1980, a fire destroyed *La Tour d'Argent,* but the owner, Sonny Lahham, in love with the cabin, had it rebuilt as close to the original as possible, and he did a very good job.

Because of its romantic atmosphere and its fine French cuisine, this restaurant attracts guests from major hotels in Houston. It is only eight minutes from the Galleria and ten minutes from the center of the city.

The exterior view is of the beautiful and well kept forest-like gardens. This is a very special view to dine by in Houston.

Windows on the Galleria

The Westin Galleria
5060 West Alabama
Houston
Texas 77056
Telephone: 713–960–8100

All major credit cards
Sunday brunch
Reservations recommended
Jacket required
Liquor served
Sunday brunch: $18 adults
*   children 12 and under: $11*
Chef: Markus Bosiger
Maitre d': Tom Wise

Only on Sunday can you have the view to dine by at Windows on the Galleria on the 24th floor of the Westin Galleria Hotel. Located in one of America's most exciting shopping malls, the famous Galleria, "Windows" offers one of the best views of the Houston skyline.

From Monday through Saturday it operates as one of Houston's top nightclubs. On Sundays it is transformed into a relaxing restaurant offering brunch at reasonable prices from 10:30 A.M. until 3 P.M.

Chef Bosiger features international selections which vary weekly, ranging from Norwegian Salmon Salad to Stuffed Onions to chicken and oyster dishes. Specials such as Snapper with Grapefruit and Fish Mousse are occasionally among the delights offered. Prime Rib and a variety of hot dishes are served as well.

Desserts and special breads, including Chocolate Mousse, Carrot Cake, Black Forest Cake, and French pastry and eclairs, are beautifully prepared here. Apple Turnover lovers will be astounded at the variety that is available.

SAN ANTONIO

The Stetson Steakhouse

Hilton Palacio del Rio
200 South Alamo Street
San Antonio
Texas 78205
Telephone: 512–222–1400

All major credit cards
Dinner
Reservations recommended
Dress: casual
Liquor served
Dinner: $12.95 to $33.95
*   full 3 courses, without wine*
Chef: Louis Spost
Maitre d': Chuck Heath

San Antonio was known to the Spanish missionaries as early as 1718, and the Spanish influence has never left. It is most apparent in its architecture, especially the many missions and the Spanish Governor's Palace. But the city's most delightful attraction, in our opinion, is the Paseo del River, the picturesque riverwalk in the downtown area. Because of the canal-type waterway, San Antonio is called the "Venice of the Southwest." The view of the riverwalk is delightful from the Stetson Steakhouse, the dining room of the Hilton Palacio del Rio.

The hotel was built in 1968—in a hurry. It was decided to have it ready in time for the Hemisfair, the Texas World Exposition of 1968. Using modules of pre-cast lightweight structural concrete, the hotel was designed and built in only 202 working days.

It wasn't until 1981 that the Stetson Steakhouse was opened in the hotel, exploiting the delightful riverwalk view. It is an excellent steak house and has received the Table Top Award. Pat O'Brien, the director of food and beverage, assures us that the beef served here is the best in all of Texas. Entrées include tender Filet Mignon, Sirloin Steak, Texas T-Bone Steak, fresh Norwegian Salmon, and New Braunfels Wiener Schnitzel—all served with Texas generosity.

UTAH
SALT LAKE CITY

The Roof

Westin Hotel Utah
Main at S. Temple
Salt Lake City
Utah 84111
Telephone: 801–531–1000

All major credit cards
Lunch and dinner
Reservations suggested
Jacket required
Liquor not served
Dinner: $14 to $22
    full 3 courses, without wine
Lunch: $5 to $9
Chef: Chuck Wiley
Maitre d': Carl Stubner

A favorite of local citizens and visitors is the rooftop restaurant on the tenth floor of the Hotel Utah. Not as high as other hotel rooftop restaurants around the country, it is nonetheless perfectly located for dramatic straight-on views of the Gothic-styled spires of the famous Mormon Temple.

The hotel is in the heart of Mormon history: a home of Brigham Young is almost next door, and in the square just across from the hotel is the Mormon Tabernacle, where on

The Roof

Thursday nights crowds of visitors go to hear the choir rehearsals and marvel at the acoustics.

There is entertainment in the Roof as well—a pianist plays familiar oldies while you dine. If you wish to drink with your meal, you must bring your own liquor. Out of respect to its neighbor, the Roof does not serve alcoholic beverages. But you may order delightful food from the menu prepared by Chef Chuck Wiley. In recent years, he has tended toward *nouvelle cuisine,* so that the food is lighter and less complex than it used to be. Among the menu favorites are the Utah Rack of Lamb. The fish is good, too—fresh and flown in from Boston the day you enjoy it. Another of the favorite dishes is Veal Oscar, a combination of veal, crab legs, and Béarnaise sauce. For something simple, try the Veal Piccata, prepared French style. *Travel/Holiday* has given the Roof awards from 1978 through 1985, and *Mobil* gave the dining room four stars. It is deserved.

VERMONT
CHITTENDEN

Mountain Top Inn
Mountain Top Road
Chittenden
Vermont 05737
Telephones: 800–445–2100 or, in Canada,
   802–483–2311

All major credit cards
Breakfast, lunch, and dinner
Reservations recommended
Jacket required for dinner
Liquor served
Dinner: $14 to $20
   full 3 courses, without wine
Lunch: $2.25 to $6.95
Chef: David Pierson
Proprietors: Jan and William Wolfe and Barbara
   and Bud McLaughlin

Mountain Top Inn, a charming country inn nestled in the Green Mountains on a 1,000 acre estate, has a spectacular panoramic view of the lake and the surrounding mountains. Each season offers a different scene—lush, verdant mountainsides in summer, an incredible mélange of foliage color in autumn, and the fantasyland of snow-covered mountains and trees in winter.

That view is enjoyed from the inn's dining room. The restaurant's interior provides an enjoyable view, too, with its post and beam construction, large exposed Douglas fir beams, an enchanting fireplace, and lovely antiques.

The inn was originally a barn but is now a full-service resort. In the 1870s the barn was part of the Long family's turnip farm. In 1940, it was purchased by William Barstow, an engineer from New York, who converted it into a wayside tavern as a hobby for his wife, Francoise. In 1945, William Wolfe and his wife Margery bought it after seeing a "for sale" advertisement in the *New York Times*. In 1955, one of its guests was President Eisenhower, who stayed here with his entourage during a fishing trip. In 1966, a ski resort was developed and, in 1979, it was completely rebuilt after a fire. This time, large windows and a glass silo staircase were added to take advantage of the views. Bill Wolfe died in 1983 but his family continues to manage the place.

The dining room's cuisine is wonderful. Among the favorites are Sautéed Bay Scallops in Dijon and Chutney as an appetizer, and, as an entrée, Stuffed Breast of Chicken with Veal Sausage in Cheddar Cheese, with McIntosh Apple Stuffing. For dessert, try the Chocolate Frangelico Cream Pie.

Not hard to find, the Mountain Top Inn is ten miles northeast of Rutland, Vermont, via Route 7 North to Chittenden Road, or via Route 4 East to Meadow Lake Drive. Follow the road to Chittenden and watch for signs directing you to the top of the mountain.

STOWE

Topnotch at Stowe

Mount Mansfield Road
P.O. Box 1260
Stowe
Vermont 05672
Telephone: 802-253-8585

All major credit cards
Breakfast and dinner, lunch in "Le Bistro"
Reservations necessary
Jacket preferred
Liquor served
Dinner: $14 to $20
full 3 courses, without wine
Lunch: $6 to $12
Chef: Anton Flory
Maitre d': Bodo Liewehr

The view from the main dining room of Topnotch at Stowe is of the resort's sculpture garden on the terrace lawn with the highest peak in Vermont, Mount Mansfield, in the background. This peak is known for offering some of the best skiing on the East Coast of the United States. What is unique about the view is that the lodge is very close to the summit and thus the view is an unobstructed one. The peak is noted for its resemblance to a giant slumbering person; the highest portion of the rock that is visible is called the "Nose"—noted for its death-defying Alpine skiing. On either side of the "Nose" are a distinct "Forehead" and "Chin."

The different seasons clearly have an impact on the nature of the mountain view as seen from the dining room. During the spring, when crocuses bloom on the terrace, the mountaintop is still covered with snow. In the fall, the brilliant colors of maples and birches intermixed with the deep greens of the coniferous forest make for an unsurpassed show of color. During the winter, the snow cover stays on the ground from late December to early April, creating a fairyland atmosphere of light, captured and accentuated in the evenings by strings of bright white lights woven through and around the barren trees surrounding the dining room. And in Vermont the light of the moon on the snow is so special that it has inspired at least one song, *Moonlight in Vermont*.

At Topnotch there are two restaurants, the main Dining Room and a small cafe called Le Bistro. The original Dining Room was a part of Topnotch when it was a small country inn, from 1950 until 1973. In 1975, the Dining Room was enlarged from about 40 to about 100 seats. In 1983, the upper tier of the Dining Room was partitioned off into the charming cafe, Le Bistro.

The Dining Room is known for its award-winning cuisine. In September 1985, at the Taste of Vermont Culinary Competition and Tasting, it won several awards. (Not surprising, given that Chef Anton Flory is one of the fifteen Master Chefs in the United States.)

Topnotch

Continental foods and original specialties of the chef are served. Among the featured items are Pheasant under Glass and venison. Selected menu items are also prepared according to the guidelines of the American Heart Association's Creative Cuisine Program (low sodium and low cholesterol). Le Bistro features a lighter menu. Both menus change seasonally.

The Trapp Family Lodge

Stowe
Vermont 05672
Telephone: 802–253–8511

All major credit cards
Breakfast, lunch, and dinner
Reservations necessary
Jacket preferred
Liquor served
Dinner: $22 prix fixe
full 3 courses, without wine
Lunch: $10 prix fixe
Chef: Michel Martinet
Maitre d': Anthony Czaja
Owner: The Von Trapp family,
General Manager: Johannes Von Trapp

Situated on 1,700 acres overlooking the Green Mountains of Vermont, the dining room of the Trapp Family Lodge has one of America's more delightful views.

In 1941 the famous Von Trapp family, immortalized in the movie *The Sound of Music*, made their American home on Luce Hill in Stowe, Vermont, in great part because the land and the breathtaking scenery reminded them of their native Austria.

In 1980, the lodge was destroyed by fire. But in December, 1983, a new world-class lodge was opened, replacing the original. From the dining room of the new lodge the view is of the broad expanse of meadows which give way to woods and, beyond, a sweeping vista of the Worcester range of the Green Mountains.

A modern 73-room hotel replaced its 27-room predecessor, still retaining the intimate charm of the original Austrian-style chalet through the use of gables, steep sloping roofs, traditionally carved balconies, and the Trapp bell tower.

The lobby is not like a hotel lobby but more like the entry hall to a private home, which, by the way, it really is: the Baroness Maria Von Trapp has her apartment here, just as she did in the original lodge.

Mostly German and Austrian food are featured here; some of the specialties are *Wienerschnitzel mit Preiselberen* (Breaded Veal Steak with Lingonberries), *Gespickter Rehschlegel* in *Rahmsauce* (Roast Leg of Venison served with a Chestnut Purée), and *Rindgulasch mit Spätzle* (Beef Goulash served with Homemade Noodles). Favorite desserts include Black Forest Cake, Apple Strudel, and Linzertorte.

The lodge dining room seats 128 people. Windsor-style chairs and tables set with white linen, candles, fresh flowers, fine china with a Blue Danube pattern, lovely silverware, and crystal glassware contribute to the beautiful interior view. The waitresses wear dirndls, and during dinner classical music is played by a harpist or guitarist.

VIRGINIA
ARLINGTON

The View Restaurant

Key Bridge Marriott Hotel
P.O. Box 9191
1401 Lee Highway
Arlington
Virginia 22209
Telephone: 703–524–6400

All major credit cards
Dinner and Sunday brunch
Reservations suggested
Jacket required
Liquor served
Dinner: $18 to $35
full 3 courses, without wine
Chefs: Donald Stern and Tony Harrington
Manager: Hamid Ghassemi

The View

The View Restaurant is on the fourteenth floor of the Key Bridge Marriott, overlooking the Potomac River and the skylines of Georgetown and Washington, D.C. In unobstructed view are the Washington Monument, the Lincoln Memorial, the Washington Cathedral, and Georgetown University. Breathtaking!

The View Restaurant, opened in 1980, was designed by Barbara Lockhart, a well-known West Coast interior designer who has decorated many homes for the rich and famous, among them Carol Burnett and William Randolph Hearst. This was the first upscale restaurant to be built in a Marriott Hotel and has served as a model for the rest of the chain. It is decorated in pink and mauve, and all of the dining chairs are individually hand carved and hand painted. Mirrored backdrops are used in the upper tier of the restaurant to provide a view for those guests seated with their backs to the view.

This restaurant was the site of Aaron Copland's 80th birthday party, with guests including Leonard Bernstein and Mstislav Rostropovich.

Among the favorites on the menu are Lobster Bisque, Zucchini-Curry Soup, Veal Medallions with Fresh Mango and Pink Peppercorns, and Fresh Poached Salmon with Vermouth Sauce. Dessert includes a daily soufflé selection served with Vanilla Haagen-Daz ice cream.

WILLIAMSBURG

For an overview of eighteenth century life in America, there is no better place than Colonial Williamsburg. From 1699 to 1780, Williamsburg was the capital of Virginia and a proving ground for both ideas and leaders. A remarkable body of men reached political maturity in Williamsburg in this era: George Washington, George Wythe, Peyton Randolph, Edmund Pendleton, Patrick Henry, George Mason, Thomas Jefferson, and a score of other Virginians. The capital proved to be an ideal setting for and a stimulus to their growth as leaders.

Inspired by Dr. W.A.R. Goodwin, Mr. John D. Rockefeller began the restoration of Williamsburg in 1926, making sure that all work was done with an eye toward recalling the fundamental principles upon which the Williamsburg of two hundred years ago made its enduring contribution to contemporary America.

Today, for all to see, Colonial Williamsburg has several major appeals to the eye and mind. They lie in its history and heritage, gardens, architecture, furniture, handcrafts, and the preservation of research in all forms, including archaeology. There is an obvious, patient concern with being authentic in every aspect, from the flowers grown and the clothing worn to the meals served.

Here, history is also a view to dine by. We've selected six of the ten delightful dining spots in Williamsburg so that you may select from among them for your view to dine by of Colonial America.

The Cascades

Visitor Center Drive
Williamsburg
Virginia 23185
Telephone: 804–229–1000

All major credit cards
Breakfast, lunch, and dinner
Reservations required
Jacket preferred
Liquor served
Dinner: $16 to $26
  full 3 courses, without wine
Lunch: $7 to $15
Chef: Charles Madison
Manager: Charles F. Trader

The area surrounding the Cascades Restaurant—beautiful woods on the grounds of the Colonial Williamsburg Visitor Center—is the place most visitors to Colonial Williamsburg go to see an orientation film, explore the shops, and study the models and exhibits so as to better understand what they will be seeing.

This is an unexpected view to dine by. A stream of water cascades into three different ponds along the side of a hill next to the restaurant. Most tables in the dining room have a view of the water.

Among the delights on the menu are a Hunt Breakfast Buffet and, at dinnertime, Scalloped Oysters, Cheese Grit Soufflé, Cheddar Cheese Soup, Seafood Brochette, and a Seafood Feast. For dessert, try the Peppermint Ice Cream.

Christiana Campbell's Tavern

Waller Street
Williamsburg
Virginia 23185
Telephone: 804–229–1000

All major credit cards
Dinner and Sunday brunch
Reservations required
Jacket preferred
Liquor served
Dinner: $16 to $26
  full 3 courses, without wine
Brunch: $8 to $11
Chef: Edward Swann

Christiana Campbell's Tavern is located on Waller Street in the historic area of Williamsburg, with a view of the grand Colonial capitol building across the street. George Washington and other leading gentlemen of the colony periodically met with local residents at this tavern. Christiana Campbell was described by a traveler in 1783 as "a little old woman, about four feet high; equally thick, a little turned up pug nose, a mouth screw'd up to one side." She was, however, an experienced tavern keeper, having learned the skill from her father.

The restaurant is delightful, with such tasty dishes as Captain Rasmussen's Clam Chowder and shrimp, lobster, and Seafood Jambalaya served with Sweet Potato Muffins. For dessert, freshly made, Rum Raisin Ice Cream is an excellent choice.

Josiah Chowning's Tavern

Duke of Gloucester Street
Williamsburg
Virginia 23185
Telephone: 804–229–1000

All major credit cards
Lunch and dinner
Reservations required
Jacket preferred
Liquor served
Dinner: $13 to $26
  full 3 courses, without wine
Lunch: $7 to $11
Chef: Manfred Roehr
Manager: Tom Kojcsich

Josiah Chowning's Tavern, in the historic area next to the Market Square, is an 18th century alehouse with informal dining. "Gambols," featuring Colonial games, entertainment, and various "diversions," occur nightly. The tavern is a typical hearty food and drink spot, just as it was two centuries ago. Among the featured items are Barbecued Pork Backribs, Barbecued Ribs of Beef, Roast Prime Rib of Beef, and Chowning's Good Bread. For dessert—apple pie, of course, unless you prefer Black Walnut Ice Cream.

The King's Arms Tavern

Duke of Gloucester Street
Williamsburg
Virginia 23185
Telephone: 804–229–1000

All major credit cards
Lunch and dinner
Reservations required
Jacket preferred
Liquor served
Dinner: $16 to $24
    full 3 courses, without wine
Lunch: $9 to $12
Chef: John Foster
Manager: Herb Harris

The King's Arms Tavern, originally owned by Mrs. Jane Vobe, was one of Williamsburg's most genteel taverns in the eighteenth century. The King's Arms, like other local taverns, served as the gathering place for discussions of politics, business, and the latest gossip. During the Revolutionary War, Mrs. Vobe and other tavern keepers supplied food, drink, and lodgings to American troops.

The cuisine specializes in traditional southern delicacies such as Virginia Peanut Soup, Sally Lunn Bread, Corn Muffins, Game Pie, and Leg of Lamb. Desserts include Pecan Pie and Fig Ice Cream.

Lodge Bay Room

South England Street
Williamsburg
Virginia 23185
Telephone: 804–229–1000

All major credit cards
Breakfast, lunch, dinner, and Sunday brunch
Reservations required
Dress: casual
Liquor served
Dinner: $15 to $25
    full 3 courses, without wine
Lunch: $3 to $9
Chef: Ted Kristengen
Maitre d': Henry Verlander

The Lodge Bay Dining Room is a spacious and sunny room furnished with green captains' chairs, butcher block tables, and luxurious carpeting. The tables are arranged near neatly paned windows and French doors to give diners a view of the immaculately manicured gardens complete with fountain, wisteria, and rocking chair-lined courtyard.

Robert Burrell's seascapes of the Chesapeake Bay area adorn the walls throughout and help create a setting for the popular seafood feast offered every Friday and Saturday night. The Sunday brunch is popular, too, with made-to-order omelets, homemade breads, and a variety of fresh fruits. Dinner, served Sunday through Thursday, features both land and sea specialties. Favorites include the Bay Overture and Crabmeat Au Gratin. The favorite dessert is Chocolate Mousse Cake.

The Regency Dining Room
at the Williamsburg Inn

Francis Street
Williamsburg
Virginia 23185
Telephone: 804–229–1000
       Ext. 2450

All major credit cards
Breakfast, lunch, and dinner
Reservations required
Jacket required
Liquor served
Dinner: $22 to $35
   full 3 courses,
    without wine
Lunch: $8 to $12
Chef: Hans J. Schadler
Maitre d': Everaud Green

The Regency Dining Room of the grand Williamsburg Inn is a rare and satisfying aesthetic and culinary experience. Tasteful surroundings of ivory and green blend with the glitter of fine silver. The view overlooks beautiful Colonial gardens and the picturesque, contemporary Golden Horseshoe Golf Course. Breakfast and lunch are served in this delightful setting.

Opened in 1937, the Williamsburg Inn is one of America's distinctly luxurious hotels. It has received numerous awards, including the *Mobil Travel Guide*'s five stars, and has played host to many VIP guests, including the monarchs of Belgium, Saudi Arabia, and Sweden, as well as prime ministers and presidents of many nations. It was the site of the 1983 Economic Summit of Industrialized Nations, hosted by President Ronald Reagan.

The cuisine here is elegant American. Among the specialties are Veal Oscar and Crabmeat Randolph.

WASHINGTON
SEATTLE

The Emerald Suite and The Space Needle Restaurant of The Space Needle

115 Warren Avenue North
Seattle
Washington 98109
Telephone: 206–447–3175

All major credit cards
Breakfast, lunch, dinner,
*   and Sunday brunch*
Reservations recommended
Jacket required in Emerald Suite
Liquor served
Dinner:
Space Needle: $13.50 to $19.25
Emerald Suite: $13.50 to $20.95
*   full 3 courses, without wine*
Lunch: Space Needle: $6.50 to $13.95
*   Emerald Suite: $7.50 to $13.95*
Chef: Steve Hartigan
Director of Food and Beverage:
*   K. Russ Goodman*

More than a million people, from all over the United States, Japan, Europe, Australia, India, and elsewhere come every year to see the view from Seattle's Space Needle.

Opened on April 21, 1962, as the dominant central structure for the 1962 Seattle World's Fair, the idea for the Space Needle was that of Edward E. Carlson, who, while relaxing in a coffee house in Stuttgart, Germany, in 1959, was inspired by the revolving restaurant in the Stuttgart Tower and began sketching his idea for a similar structure that he proposed to build in Seattle.

When completed, the Space Needle was the engineering feat of the day. Its underground foundation weighed as much as the Needle itself and established the center of gravity at just above ground level. The steel erection used massive and unusually shaped members to form slender legs and the tophouse. The five-level dome was completed with special attention to the revolving restaurants and an observation deck.

Storms have forced the closing of the Space Needle only twice, once on Columbus Day of 1962, when winds from a storm gusted as high as 83 miles per hour, and again in 1973 during 75-mile-an-hour winds. However, the Needle was built to withstand high wind velocity, and it has withstood several earthquake tremors, including one in 1965 that measured a healthy 6.5 on the Richter scale.

The view from over 500 feet is a 360-degree panorama of striking Pacific Northwest scenery—the Olympic and Cascade Mountain ranges, Mount Rainier, the downtown Seattle waterfront, the Port of Seattle, Puget Sound, and Lake Union.

Eighteen feet below the observation deck is the revolving restaurant level. There the Space Needle Restaurant serves fine food in an informal setting and the Emerald Suite offers elegant dining. Both feature Pacific Northwest cuisine, emphasizing fresh seafood and produce (from the fabulous Pike Place Market of Seattle), with Continental flourishes. The cuisine has been judged "exceptional" by *Pacific Northwest* magazine and has received several "Best in the West" awards from *PSA* magazine. Among the notable items on the menu are Seattle Stew, Space Needle Seafood Chowder, and Space Needle Apple Pie. Our favorite is the Dungeness Crab.

Through the years the restaurants here had many honored guests, including John Glenn, Prince Philip of Great Britain, Russian cosmonaut Gherman Titov, King Hussein of Jordan, the Shah and Empress of Iran, and many governors, vice-presidents, presidents, and movie and theatrical stars.

The King of Tonga was probably the Needle's heaviest visitor. He weighed 400 pounds and had to have a special chair carried up the service elevator.

WASHINGTON, D.C.

The Mayfair Restaurant

The Grand Hotel
2350 M Street, N.W.
Washington
District of Columbia 20037
Telephone: 202–429–0100 Ext. 4488

All major credit cards
Lunch and dinner
Reservations necessary
Jacket required
Liquor served
Dinner: $30 to $40
    full 3 courses, without wine
Lunch: $12 to $18
Chef: Richard J. Hill
Maitre d': Christian Mattei

A very distinguished new hotel with a European flavor, the Grand Hotel is reminiscent of some of Europe's superb small hotels. Although scaled to the baroque grandeur of the nation's capital, the Grand Hotel of Washington has the intimacy, charm, and elegance of a private mansion.

Located in Washington's West End, formerly the industrial area of the city, the building's Skidmore, Owings, and Merrill design gives it an air of timelessness. The Grand Hotel projects the monumental character of Washington with its copper-topped dome wedged between the corners of the building. The gray brick, granite, and concrete blocks of the building's exterior fit within the monumental scale yet are proportioned to impart a neighborhood residential feeling.

The lobby has double columns ringing its rotunda, resulting in a circular lounge area crowned by a 16-foot stepped dome. The graceful marble staircase leads to the Promenade and to the European-style interior courtyard.

This beautifully landscaped courtyard is the view to dine by from the Mayfair restaurant. A special sight is the wall-mounted fountain from which water cascades down a series of basins to the collecting pool below. There is also a stillwater pond stocked with eye-catching tropical fish.

Located off the lobby, the restaurant seats 110 people and is a pleasant setting for lunch or dinner.

The restaurant's dominant colors are warm tones of peach, deep coral, and camel. Peach silk covers the ceiling with a delicate shimmer of color, and the carpeting is patterned in deep coral and camel. The deep coral tone is repeated in the upholstery of the comfortable banquettes. Gold leaf covers the frames and the seating of traditional side chairs, accenting the Fortuny covering of white shot with pure gold. White linen tablecloths are a crisp setting for elegant china, silver, and crystal, as well as colorful floral arrangements.

The focal point of the room is the ceiling's dome. Beveled mirrors line the walls, reflecting the individual table lamps, the indirect light of the dome, and the courtyard. During the day, ambient light enters through the curved bank of French windows that open to the view of the courtyard and its gardens.

The Mayfair features French Continental cuisine exquisitely presented. While the menu for lunch and dinner is the same, the lunch menu is enhanced with daily special selections. The most popular and innovative specialties on the menu include Navarin of Lobster with Baby Vegetables, Lamb Noisettes with Truffle and Parsley, Salmon Quenelles with Morels and Herbs, and Veal Medallions with Shittakes and Roasted Shallots. Many writers are moved to say two things about the Mayfair: "it is the most beautiful restaurant room in the United States" and "its cooking rates with that of the finest restaurants in Washington."

WISCONSIN
MILWAUKEE

Polaris Restaurant and Cocktail Lounge

Hyatt Regency Milwaukee
333 West Kilbourn Avenue
Milwaukee
Wisconsin 53203
Telephone: 414–276–1234

All major credit cards
Lunch and dinner
Reservations not required
Jacket not required
Liquor served
Dinner: $10.95 to $18.50
    full 3 courses, without wine
Lunch: $4.25 to $6.50
General Manager: Keith Mangum

Here is the spot from which to see all of Milwaukee. The Polaris Restaurant and Cocktail Lounge are in a revolving dome 22 stories atop the Hyatt Regency Milwaukee.

The 360-degree view of the city, including much of the surrounding area and beautiful Lake Michigan, takes about an hour to see completely as the restaurant revolves.

Although it does attract tourists, the Polaris is the local favorite for celebrations ranging from weddings to anniversary parties. There is no other restaurant like it in Milwaukee.

Favorite times to visit Polaris and enjoy the view are at sunset, during a light evening snowfall (when the view appears to be a beautiful impressionist painting), and whenever there are fireworks for festive and holiday events.

Lunch is served from 11:30 A.M. until 2 P.M. Monday through Friday, and its offerings include salads, sandwiches, and entrées ranging from $4.25 to $7.50 (for Prime Rib *au Jus* —English-cut prime rib of beef on a French loaf with fried onions, served with creamy horseradish and natural juices). A favorite is Milwaukee *En Vuelo* (twin enchiladas topped with sauce ranchero, cheddar cheese, and sour cream, served with refried beans, Spanish rice, guacamole, tortilla chips, and sauce caliente).

Dinner is served every night from 5:30 P.M. until 10 P.M., and entrées include Roast Duck, Lobster Tail, BBQ Ribs, Chinese Walnut Chicken, Chicken Normandy, Baked Lasagna, seasonal fresh fish, and Prime Ribs of Beef *au Jus*. Entrées range from $10.95 to $18.50. A modest dessert selection includes a local favorite, Apple Strudel, and our favorites, Carrot Cake and Mud Pie.

WYOMING
GRAND TETON NATIONAL PARK

Mural Dining Room

Jackson Lake Lodge
Grand Teton National Park
P.O. Box 250
Moran
Wyoming 83013
Telephone: 307–543–2811

All major credit cards
Breakfast, lunch, and dinner
Reservations recommended
Jacket not required
Liquor served
Dinner: $14.25 to $23.75
full 3 courses, without wine
Lunch: $6.55 to $10
Chef: Robert L. Walton

The best of the places to eat in Jackson Lake Lodge is the Mural Dining Room, not only because of its extensive menu, but also because of the scenery it offers.

The Mural Dining Room is so named because its walls are covered with murals based on the work of artist Alfred Jacob Miller, who in 1837 made watercolor sketches as he traveled with Captain William Drummond Stewart on a fur trading expedition. Miller's sketches were converted to today's murals by Carl Roters; they depict scenes from a trapper's life, such as camping under the Tetons and the annual trading fair where trappers exchange their pelts for the supplies they need to survive in the wilderness.

The dining room features popular American cuisine. Among the specialties are Smoked Trout, vegetarian dinners, Prime Rib, fresh pastries, and fresh strawberries. You share the dining room with guests from all parts of the United States as well as from many parts of the world.

Index of Restaurants